# The Arizona Governors

# 1912—1990

The publisher and authors received documents, photographs and held personal interviews during the research and collection of the material for this publication that were provided by others and verification of data was either impossible or limited regarding dates, places, correct names and events. Every reasonable effort was exercised to ascertain the correctness and substantiate the information. However, some information was presented as received and may need validation or correction. Therefore, the publisher assumes no liability for information and data received that could not be validated to the best of its ability.

# The Arizona Governors

# 1912—1990

Dr. John L. Myers
Editor-in-Chief

Heritage Publishers, Inc.
Phoenix, Arizona

**Heritage Publishers Staff:**

Dr. John L. Myers, President and Editor-in-Chief
Karen K. Kroman, Managing Editor
Dr. Robert Gryder, Senior Editor
Isabelle Blanco-Castro, Assistant Editor
Lynne Atkinson, Production Coordinator
Robert John Gryder, Assistant Production Coordinator
Steve Benson, Political Cartoonist
Vanessa Davisson, Layout and Design Artist
Cynthia J. Matthews, Publishing Board
Ty L. Myers, Publishing Board
Lorrie E. Maddux, Publishing Board

**Authors:**

Anna Laura Bennington
Nelda C. Garcia
John S. Goff
Robert Gryder
Margaret Finnerty
Marianne M. Jennings
David H. Lynch
Richard E. Lynch
Karen K. Kroman
Christine N. Marin
Donald J. Tate

## The Arizona Governors
## 1912—1990

Published by

Heritage Publishers, Inc.
4633 North 30th Place
Phoenix, Arizona  85016
(602) 468-9143

Library of Congress Catalog Number:  89-80719.
ISBN 0-929690-05-2

Printed in the United States of America

# Contents

# FOREWORD

She is all of these: young, beautiful, and exciting. She is Arizona—the 48th state in the United States of America. After territorial controversy and a rather lengthy waiting period, she was born on February 14, 1912. Since then she has attracted many visitors and residents. Her beauty is unsurpassed; it should remain her most treasured quality.

The Organic Act of February 24, 1864, signed by President Abraham Lincoln, established the Arizona Territory. Early territorial history documented Arizona as a place where few visited because of harsh weather, rugged terrain, and rampaging Indian tribes. Early Spanish explorers discovered vast lands, precious mineral deposits, and mixed agricultural use of the soil.

As speculators, miners, ranchers, and military outposts sprang up, more settlers became aware of the spectacular wonders of Arizona. With the establishment of the stage, telegraph and railroad lines, and rapidly increasing mining camps, Arizona attracted many people who fell in love with her and began to tell others stories about their new found love affair.

In the early years of the twentieth century, the population began to grow. Increasing demands for services were expected by her new residents. With a variety of individual interests and needs to be met in a territory of unclaimed lands, a political movement surfaced to become a governed state. With men and women who were known for their endurance and determination, it was not too long before territorial residents became organized and leaders emerged to address the many issues to be resolved.

In 1912, statehood was approved. One of the first leaders to become governor was George W. P. Hunt. Since that time Arizona has elected seventeen governors who led her to become the proud state she is today. This leadership has not always been easy nor without controversy. History records that each governor has provided Arizona with leadership qualities that appeared necessary for the time and the particular stage in her development.

Arizona residents, students of all ages, and visitors know little about the leadership that has provided direction for Arizona in past decades. Arizona Governors have included seventeen men and one woman with experience from the business world, professional fields, and political careers. Each of these individuals has been interesting and driven by the determination to make a difference. Each governor added strength to the developmental process of our young state. What one learns from political history will, hopefully, benefit future political leadership.

This is Arizona's first book to be published about all eighteen of Arizona's governors. The governors faced many critical issues; each one made a contribution to this state. Those who have lived and shared this history recognize the importance for others to learn more about each of our state's governors. This knowledge could lead to a better understanding and to a need for further research.

The Arizona Governors 1912-1990 is another first for Arizona. This book will enhance the interest to learn more about the political experiences and processes that have affected this great state. The seven living governors, historians, contributing authors, and residents of Arizona have made this book possible. To all who have contributed, we extend our respectful appreciation. We salute the Arizona Governors who gave of themselves that others could enjoy her many wonders. Arizona has been blessed with her history of political leadership. My wish is that Arizona history continue to record excellence in her political leadership as she moves toward the twenty-first century.

Dr. John L. Myers

**The Capitol Building, State of Arizona**
**Credit: Arizona Department of Library**
**Archives and Public Records**

# ACKNOWLEDGEMENTS

This book, that covers approximately eighty years of Arizona political leadership, would have been impossible without the cooperation and assistance from many people. The idea was first introduced to the current Governor and her support was important for the initial idea to become reality. Governor Rose Mofford and her staff were most helpful and needed in order for this project to become a reference tool for residents of today and tomorrow.

In order for this book to be researched, written, and published, the public was invited to participate in the first Arizona Governors' Banquet which was held on May 19, 1989, at Camelback Inn. To all who attended, including individuals and corporate sponsors, your interest and support was critical. Participants in this important event who made the evening significant included the Master of Ceremonies, Mr. C. E. "Pep" Cooney, President and General Manager of KPNX Channel 12, the Honorable Congressman John J. Rhodes, Governor Rose Mofford, and the political cartoonist Mr. Steve Benson who drew the political cartoons of each governor who appears in this publication. In attendance were five of the living governors: Governor Rose Mofford, Governor Evan Mecham, Governor Raul H. Castro, Governor Samuel P. Goddard, and Governor Paul J. Fannin. Their participation, along with their families and family members of other former governors, was truly appreciated. Mrs. Donna Roe, Manager of Catering for Camelback Inn, delivered an elegant setting that all in attendance enjoyed and appreciated. This historic event was supported by members of the Phoenix Forty with special assistance from Mr. William Shover and Mr. Jerry Witkowsky.

The research for this publication was greatly assisted by the staff of the Research Division, Department of Library, Archives, and Public Records, State of Arizona, the cooperation of the library staff at Arizona State University, Mr. William Shover and his staff at *The Arizona Republic/The Phoenix Gazette,* and living Governors of Arizona.

All of the contributing authors performed their research and writing in a professional manner that made the text come alive. Their professional contribution and commitment was significant and invaluable. The staff of Historical Publishers and Heritage Publishers performed each task as anticipated in a manner that proved extremely important for this publication. Ms. Vanessa Davisson gave special care to insure that the layout and design was appropriate for this historic publication and performed that task exceptionally well.

To all who were a part of this important process, my sincere appreciation. To those who will have the opportunity to enjoy and learn from this publication, I trust you will gain insight and knowledge that will be helpful in your understanding of our Governors of Arizona. The leadership of each former governor has been important for Arizona to grow and develop in order that she best serve her people. We trust that the leadership of future governors and the understanding of the future residents will have been served well through this publication.

# The Arizona Governors' Banquet
## May 19, 1989

# The Arizona Governors' Banquet
## May 19, 1989

**Governor George W. P. Hunt**
**Credit: Arizona Department of Library**
**Archives and Public Records**

# GEORGE W. P. HUNT

## 1912—1917, 1917—1919
## 1923—1929, 1931—1933

*Author: Dr. John S. Goff*

The first governor of the state of Arizona was unique in several ways. No other individual, it is safe to say, will ever be elected governor seven times by the people. Those two-year terms which are no longer used meant that Hunt was in office most of the time over a twenty-year period. It might be well to begin by describing this remarkable individual. He stood about five feet nine inches in height and weighed close to three hundred pounds. Totally bald, he had not a hair on his head, but wore a handle-bar mustache which at times was waxed and stuck out beyond his ears, while later in life the mustache drooped and he called himself the "Old Walrus."

There is no agreement about Hunt's names. George was certain and P. undoubtedly signified Paul although relatives called him Pearle; it was the W. that is uncertain. At various times in his life it was Willie, Wiley, Wyley and Wylley. Newspaper cartoonists at times insisted he was "George Washington Peter Hunt."

Born November 1, 1859, in Huntsville, Missouri, a town named for his family, his father was George Washington Hunt, a forty-niner who did not find California to his liking and returned to the Midwest. His mother, Sarah Elizabeth (Yates) Hunt, was a writer and a poet. Although the family had once been well-to-do, all of that was swept away by the Civil War and Hunt remembered that his family was desperately poor. The boy was educated in local schools, public and private. Once he failed a course because he could not afford to buy a textbook; long afterward he remembered and championed free books for students in the Arizona public schools.

March 3, 1878, was an important day in his life. Early that morning he ran away from home. He was not close to his father but hated to leave his mother. Long afterward he would arrange to have a little book of her poems published. For three years the family thought he had been killed by Indians. Instead he wandered across Kansas, spent some time in Colorado, floated down the Rio Grande on a raft, and came into Arizona searching for a lost mine. Early in October, 1881, Hunt walked into the town of Globe, dressed in overalls and leading a burro. Globe would be his symbolic, if not his actual home, for the rest of his life.

The first job Governor Hunt had in his new home town was as a waiter in a restaurant. The couple who owned Pascoe's became his friends for life. In succeeding years he worked as a "mucker" in the Old Dominion Mine, tried cattle ranching, and had various other odd jobs. During the Summer of 1890, when he was past thirty years of age, Hunt got a job as a delivery boy with the A. Bailey and Company, a general store. It merged into what became the Old Dominion Commercial Company and ten years later, Hunt was its president. The Governor always said, "My best experience was my business training." Early in his career he had operated the grocery department and for the rest of his life he often did the shopping for his own household. His business career made him a moderately wealthy man but when he became governor he sold his stock in the company and thereafter only invested in government bonds.

The first time the name George W. P. Hunt appeared on an Arizona ballot was when he ran for Gila County Recorder in 1890. He lost. Two years later he was nominated to run for the territorial house of representatives and this time he won over both the Republican and Populist nominees. As a freshman member of the legislature in 1893, he was well regarded and won approval from the press in the capital city. After briefly serving as Gila County

**Governor and Mrs. Hunt**

Treasurer, Hunt went back to the legislature again in 1895 and in 1897 and 1899 served in the council, as the upper chamber of the legislature was called. A great admirer of William Jennings Bryan, Hunt was a populist in all but name and supported the democratic reforms of that era such as votes for women, the income tax, the secret ballot, compulsory school laws and the free coinage of silver.

By his own choice Governor Hunt did not run for office between 1898 and 1904 although he remained active in Democratic party politics. He was busy with his work and was becoming well known throughout the territory. Hunt was married in Holbrook, February 24, 1904, and settled into family life. The First Lady was born near Eagle Springs, Texas, November 10, 1867, the daughter of Jesse W. and Susan (Smith) Ellison. Her name was Helen Duett Ellison and her husband called her by her middle name. The family settled in Gila County and Duett was raised on a ranch. Hunt first met her in 1890 but being the dutiful daughter she was always needed at home and the marriage was often postponed. The couple had one daughter, Virginia.

Surviving letters show that after her marriage, Mrs. Hunt was not only busy with ranch and family matters but largely ran the Old Dominion Commercial Company while her husband was busy with politics in Phoenix. It is said that she was the model for some of Zane Grey's heroines and while later people could and did criticize the Governor, the First Lady was beloved by everyone. She had those qualities of character which typified the frontier woman and was modest and retiring in addition. Not especially interested in "society" matters, she nevertheless was always a gracious hostess and a loving and caring individual.

Hunt returned to public life in the election of 1904 when he was again elected to the council and in January, 1905, was elected its president when it assembled. The session proved disappointing to the man from Gila County as his proposal to adopt the direct primary system of nominating candidates to public office failed of adoption. At the next legislative session two years later, Hunt was a little more pleased. A new tax law on the mines was enacted and his bill to outlaw gambling in the territory won the approval of President Theodore Roosevelt. The last

territorial legislature, the Twenty-Fifth, met in January, 1909, and Hunt was again elected president. The primary law was finally enacted and Hunt was active in the creation of the Pioneers' Home in Prescott. Everyone was aware of the fact that statehood was imminent, something much advocated by George W. P. Hunt.

Admission into the Union was something the people of Arizona had worked toward for several decades. At last in June of 1910, the Congress passed the Enabling Act which would allow the calling of an election to select delegates to a constitutional convention. When it was held, fifty-two men (women did not yet have political rights) were chosen to be "founding fathers"; forty-one of them were Democrats and eleven Republicans. One of the five delegates from Gila County was George W. P. Hunt. The convention assembled in the capitol at noon on October 9, 1910, and his colleagues elected him president. One of the long-lived men who served recalled many years later that it was reasonably safe to say that few items went into the constitution without the approval of President Hunt.

The writing of Arizona's only fundamental charter took two months and then it was approved by the people and by the Congress. However, President Taft insisted that the recall of judges be removed before he would sign the statehood resolution. George W. P. Hunt was a strong supporter of the recall, the initiative and referendum and what he called the "progressive" features of the constitution. For the rest of his life he would strongly defend what he and his colleagues had created. At last, on February 14, 1912, the Flood Resolution was signed by the Chief Executive and conferred statehood on the forty-eighth member of the Federal Union.

The achievement of statehood came at the peak of the Progressive era, an important reform movement of the early twentieth century; unlike Populism earlier, the progressives were more practical and substantial individuals. Theodore Roosevelt best stated their philosophy when he declared that "unless we make the United States a reasonably good place for all its people, it will very soon cease to be a good place for any of them." Hunt subscribed to that notion and insisted he always had faith in the people. What the nation needed was more democracy.

**Governor Hunt on the Campaign Trail, 1926**

**(left to right) Governor Hunt and President Franklin D. Roosevelt
September 26, 1932**

Those who opposed change and supported the *status quo* called Hunt a socialist, and even worse; but he continued to denounce intrenched wealth and the "big interests" as he called them. The latter was a polite term, for one newspaper noted that in a campaign he began referring to the big interests, the stand-patters and the reactionaries, and by the end of the race they had become coyotes, jackals and skunks.

The elections to select the first officials of the new state of Arizona were held in the Fall of 1911, first the primary and then the general election. In September, George W. P. Hunt announced that we would seek the governorship and he won the Democratic primary and then narrowly defeated the Republican candidate, Judge Edmund W. Wells, of Prescott. On inauguration day Hunt announced that since he had walked into Arizona he would walk to the capitol. He did but one of his critics noted that it was about the last time the portly chief executive was ever known to use that method of locomotion.

The new state legislature met in March and its regular session was followed by three special sessions; all state laws were revised as the code had not been reworked since 1901. The governor had no hesitation in telling the lawmakers what he wanted including anti-child labor laws, an anti-usury law, a law which would require newspapers to disclose their stockholders, an anti-lobbying law, old age pensions and workers' compensation laws. He was especially firm in his opposition to capital punishment and when speaking of the need for prison reform he insisted that the only difference between those in jail and those out was that the jailed group had been caught and the others hadn't —yet!

The Arizona Supreme Court ruled that there would be no elections for state officials in 1912 and so Hunt did not face the voters until 1914. Then he defeated both the Republican nominee Ralph H. Cameron and the Progressive candidate, George U. Young, to win a second term. By this time events outside Arizona intruded upon the new state. Mexico was in turmoil and the great war in Europe began. Once the United States entered the latter conflict, Hunt took up knitting scarves for soldiers as apart of his patriotic duty and told a recruiter he wished he could join the Marines. When a Flagstaff resident questioned his

support of the war, he sued for libel and collected one cent in damages. Politics was a rough business even then.

In 1916, Hunt's opponent was the popular Thomas E. Campbell and he worried over the outcome of the election. He had good reason to do so and there followed a disputed election. Leaving matters to the courts, Hunt surrendered his office on January 27, 1917. This year was a troubled one in Arizona with labor strikes getting much attention. On July 2, President Wilson asked his Arizona friend to serve as a federal labor conciliator and Hunt looked at it differently. Of the mine owners he wrote in his diary, "I try to stand for Justice— they want to run things." He was a little embarrassed when his photograph was printed after the raiding of the offices of the I. W. W., considered a radical union. The real problem was that he loved to have his picture taken, with anyone, anytime.

After a year of legal battles, George W. P. Hunt was restored to the governor's office on Christmas Day 1917, the result of a unanimous opinion by the state supreme court. He served out the term but decided not to run for re-election in 1918. Once out of office he was bored. He tried to learn to drive but after the car wound up in the ditch a few times he gave up, noting in his diary that life was like an automobile ride: "One started out in the morning with exhilaration and by nightfall was towed home in humiliation." It seemed likely that Hunt would run for the United States Senate which was the last thing United States Senator Mark Smith wanted. In all probability, it was Smith who arranged something for Hunt.

In February, 1920, the people of the state were very surprised to learn that President Wilson had nominated George W. P. Hunt to be United States Minister to Siam. The nominee made his preparations to go to Asia despite the fact that one man who had held the post some years before told him he would never survive the duty. He did and had a wonderful time. Mrs. Hunt and their daughter, Virginia, spent a few months there but returned for her schooling. Hunt found there was little work to be done so he explored the country, described a banquet given him by the King as "some big feed," and sent presents and postcards to the voters at home. They were very impressed. Hunt's diplomatic career

**Governor Hunt in his Office**
**February 24, 1925**
**Credit: Arizona Department of Library**
**Archives and Public Records**

**Governor Hunt Knitting
for the Soldiers at War
Credit: Arizona Department of Library
Archives and Public Records**

ended in September, 1921, when the new Republican President sent a new minister to replace him. The Arizonan toured the world before coming home. Upon his arrival in Phoenix, Hunt visited schools dressed in Siamese costume and spoke to many groups. Before long the talks centered less about his experiences in far way lands and more about Arizona politics. By the Spring of 1922, Hunt was in the race for governor again and that November he defeated Governor Campbell and took office again in January, 1923. Few realized it at the time but it would be six years before he left the capitol again. In very close races in 1924 and 1926, he defeated two very able Republican nominees, Dwight B. Heard and Elias S. Clark.

From 1923 to 1929, Governor Hunt battled for those causes he had supported in earlier years. It is curious that he could be so reform minded and at the same time operated like an old fashioned machine politician. If one held a state office, it was absolutely required that one donate a month's salary every two years to finance the next campaign. Except for the battle over the waters of the Colorado River, the roaring twenties were relatively quiet ones for the governor. He often learned that the old statement, that in Arizona the governor proposes and the legislature disposes, was very true.

The water issue came to the fore after World War I as southern California began to look for water and electrical power to support its growth. Governor Hunt argued correctly that our neighboring state contributed almost nothing to the Colorado River and demanded much more than its fair share of what he called "Arizona's birthright." The whole matter involved seven states, the federal government, and the Republic of Mexico. The 1923 Santa Fe Compact had planned for the apportionment of the water but Hunt vehemently opposed it. There is a joke from that time to the effect that while Jesus walking on water was a miracle, it was not so amazing as the Governor of Arizona who regularly ran on the Colorado! Nevertheless Hoover Dam was built after Congress passed the hated Sing-Johnson Act in the latter part of 1928. Hunt vowed to continue the fight in the courts.

When Hunt made his usual race for governor in 1928, he was nearly seventy years of age and had been in office a long time. Even some supporters wondered if he would ever retire. On a visit to Phoenix, Will Rogers met Hunt at the airport and asked him how his "hereditary governorship" was working out and might Hunt adopt Rogers so he could succeed him. The year 1928 was a Republican year and Hunt was defeated by that party's candidate, John C. Phillips. The former governor made a trip around the world to get himself occupied. Starting in the Fall of 1929, the United States began to experience the worst depression ever known. George W. P. Hunt was genuinely saddened by the hard times and it took little coaxing by his friends to persuade him to run again. He narrowly defeated Governor Phillips and in January, 1931, was sworn into office for what proved to be his final term.

His health was poor and once or twice his life was threatened. On April 18, 1931, he suffered the great tragedy of his life. Mrs. Hunt died from minor surgery and he was left without his helpmate. He never recovered. A monument to the First Lady, a white pyramid, was constructed in Papago Park where ultimately the family would be entombed. Hunt in a note said he wanted to be buried on a spot where, as he put it, his spirit would overlook the land where the people truly ruled.

The depression could not be solved by the governor, or the legislature, and Hunt gradually came to accept the idea that the federal government must act. Traditionally he had been a state's rights Democrat but welcomed Franklin D. Roosevelt's New Deal. Events happened which troubled the old man. So many people were out of work. There was a veterans' march on Washington and the west coast marchers stopped in Phoenix on their way east. Hunt ordered loaves of bread and medicine and paid for the items out of his own pocket. He saw little light ahead.

In the 1932 Democratic primary Hunt was defeated for the first time in his life and the event was repeated two years later. Dr. Benjamin B. Moeur had ended his political career. The old man hoped for a diplomatic appointment from the Roosevelt administration but it did not materialize. People in trouble called at the Hunt home and an associate often saw the old man press a ten or twenty dollar bill into the hand of those who had helped him in happier days. He died at his Phoenix home, which he had built in 1915, on December 24,

1934. A remarkable man had passed from the scene.

George W. P. Hunt was the major figure in state politics during the first quarter century after admission. He frustrated several political careers by holding office so long. The secret of his success as a politician was that he never made permanent enemies. A person or a group might split off and go over to the opposition, but a few years later they might well be back in the fold. He was a master politician. An aide recalled that he would be sent to the grocery to buy several cases of jams and jellies. Labels would be washed off and when the Governor went out to Sunday dinner with a family of voters he would take a jar of jelly or jam out of his pocket and present it to the lady of the household with the comment, "My wife was making jam the other day and she wanted you to have this . . . ."

## SOURCES

*Dictionary of American Biography*

"George W. P. Hunt," *Arizona Biographical Series*, Cave Creek, Black Mountain Press, 1987

Goff, John S., *George W. P. Hunt and His Arizona*, Pasadena, California, Socio-Technical Publications, 1973

*The National Cyclopedia of American Biography*

*Who Was Who in America, 1897—1942*

Collection of Governor Hunt's newspaper clippings, The University of Arizona

Diary of George W. P. Hunt, Arizona State University, Tempe, Arizona

The Arizona Department of Library, Archives and Public Records owns his unpublished autobiography

**Governor Thomas E. Campbell**
**Credit: Arizona Department of Library**
**Archives and Public Records**

# THOMAS E. CAMPBELL

**1917**
**1919—1923**

*Author: Dr. John S. Goff*

Governor Campbell was not only the first native born Governor of Arizona but one of the relatively few who had that distinction. Christened Thomas Edward Campbell, he was born on the grounds of Ft. Whipple, adjacent to Prescott, January 18, 1878. His father, "Dashing Dan," more formally known as Daniel E. Campbell, was a native of Philadelphia. Orphaned and reared by an aunt at the age of sixteen or seventeen, he ran away from home and joined the army. While stationed at Fort Scott, Kansas, he met Elizabeth Flynn, from County Sligo, Ireland, and two and a half months younger than he. They married and eventually had seven children. Mrs. Campbell did not like the idea of moving about the frontier and so persuaded her husband to resign from the army and settle in Prescott.

The Governor's parents operated the first dairy in town, and later owned a grocery store and lived on Alarcon Street. Both lived long full lives; she reached eighty and he eighty-seven years. Young Tom went to St. Mary's Catholic School and in 1896 graduated from Prescott High School. He wanted to attend the University of California but one was required to be proficient in both Latin and Greek and those subjects were not offered by the Prescott schools. Instead, he attended St. Mary's College near Oakland, California, for one year.

When the Spanish-American War broke out, the young man wanted to join the Rough Riders but his mother was very much opposed and the father agreed with her. Instead, he became assistant postmaster in Prescott but very shortly was put in charge of the post office in Jerome. He and a partner also operated a tobacco shop. He also joined the town volunteer fire department and was elected captain. Insofar as a life-long career was concerned, he never had any doubts. Always interested in mining, he became a mining engineer. When still young, he developed a claim to the extent that he was able to sell it to William Andrew Clark for $10,000.

During the Summer of 1899, Campbell met (Eleanor) Gayle Allen, the daughter of Henry J. and Annabelle (Wright) Allen. Born in Shreveport, Louisiana, February 9, 1878, her father was the office manager of the United Verde mining operations and an influential man in the community. She had returned home following her graduation from Mills College in California and the couple was married in Jerome on June 8, 1900. Two sons, Allen and Brodie, would in time complete the family circle. Intelligent and educated, the future First Lady was not only a full partner in her husband's career but was as active in the social life of the places where they lived as her family obligations would permit. On occasion she would substitute for the Governor at ceremonial events when his schedule would not permit his being there in person.

The Campbells had never been especially active in politics but "Tom," as everyone called him, was a great admirer of Alexander O. Brodie, West Point graduate, Rough Rider commander and later Governor of Arizona by the appointment of his friend Theodore Roosevelt. Brodie persuaded Campbell to run for the legislature which he did in 1900. The young man was successful and not only was he the youngest member of the 1901 House of Representatives but he was also the first native Arizonan to be a lawmaker. His most important proposal was one to limit underground miners to an eight-hour work day. The bill passed the House but was not adopted in the Council.

**Thomas Campbell in the Front Harness as Fire Chief
and Captain of the Jerome Fire Department Team
of 1899
Credit: Arizona Historical Society Library, Tucson**

**Young Thomas E. Campbell**
**Credit: Arizona Historical Society Library**

In the years following his return home from the Capitol, Campbell was postmaster of Jerome, agent for the Yavapai Indians and busy locating likely mining sites. Eventually, the family moved to Prescott. A new law of 1907 authorized the board of supervisors to appoint a county assessor. Thomas E. Campbell was selected for Yavapai County, and when under the state constitution the office was made elective, he retained his office at the polls. His duties made him responsible for seeing that all property, real and personal, was placed on the tax rolls so that it would pay its proper share of the costs of running the government. Many days of horseback riding were required to fulfill the duties of the office but he was very successful and was elected president of the Arizona Assessor's Association.

Although the courts had ruled there would be no state elections in 1912, it was still necessary for Representative Carl Hayden to face the voters, and Campbell, as the Republican nominee for the lower house of Congress, ran not only against Hayden but also Progressive, Socialist and Prohibitionist nominees. The Republican finished a respectable third in a contest where the outcome could easily have been predicted ahead of time. Carl Hayden would remain in office for a long time to come.

The first state legislature created the Arizona Tax Commission, and considering his experiences, it was logical that Campbell should be his party's choice for a position on it. He ran in 1914 and was elected, taking office in January, 1915. Not being a wealthy man and in need of funds to help support his family, he also at this time operated a ranch on the upper Verde, assisted by family members and employees. Government salaries in those days were not very lucrative. Campbell's work on the tax commission brought him into contact with many people and almost at once he was being talked of as a Republican candidate for governor. In those days the Democrats were the majority group but this man was able to win voters over to his side. Even Governor Hunt conceded: "Mr. Campbell was a fine, prepossessing gentleman, and a good campaigner. He was of striking appearance, in his ten gallon hat."

The 1916 election ended in a dispute. Hunt thought he was defeated by Campbell and would not claim victory. By November 23, it was reported in the press that Campbell was ahead by 55 votes. Early in December, Hunt demanded a recount and that took nearly a month in the Maricopa County Superior Court of Judge R. C. Stanford. Beginning in January, 1917, Arizona had two governors and on the 27th, the state supreme court ruled that Campbell should be recognized as *de facto* chief executive until matters were finally settled. He took charge of the governor's office on the morning of the 29th. When he addressed the assembled legislators, he had several recommendations, two of which were major reforms. He urged that the state adopt an executive budget system, a matter not realized until the Goddard Administration. Campbell also felt limiting the state debt to $350,000 was inadequate and should be changed to "an amount commensurate with the needs of a growing state." That has not been realized to this date.

The Great War began in the Spring of 1917 and Governor Campbell mobilized the state and its citizens to do everything possible to aid the cause. He was made chairman of the Arizona Red Cross and the First Lady traveled about the state urging the purchase of Liberty Bonds. To compound difficulties, the serious labor unrest which had troubled the state for many months became more of an issue. There were strikes at Jerome, Globe and Bisbee. The latter resulted in the infamous Bisbee Deportation which took place in mid-July. Nearly 1,400 individuals were loaded into railroad freight cars by the Citizens' Protective League and hauled over into Mexico. The Governor visited the scene and said he would remain there until county officials pledged to remain within the law and the situation was quieted.

On May 2, Judge Stanford ruled that Campbell was the rightful winner of the disputed election and remained so convinced the rest of his life. However, immediately an appeal was taken and in October argument was heard by the justices. Finally, on the morning of December 22, 1917, the court unanimously ruled that George W. P. Hunt had been duly elected governor in the preceding general election. Thomas E. Campbell turned the office over to George W. P. Hunt; he had served nearly a year and all without salary. Additionally, he was responsible for the legal fees and the court costs the dispute had

**Governor Thomas E. Campbell**
**Credit: Arizona Department of Library**
**Archives and Public Records**

**Governor and Mrs. Thomas Campbell**
**Credit: Arizona Historical Society Library, Tucson**

generated.

It came as a surprise to no one when in May, 1918, Campbell announced that he would again run for governor. Hunt was retiring and the Democrats chose Fred T. Colter as their candidate. For the only time in Arizona history, two native sons battled for the state's highest office. The general election results of November 5, 1918, were so close that the results were in doubt for several days. At last, it was known that Campbell had won by fewer than 400 votes. The new governor spent the remaining weeks of the year in preparing for his inauguration to be held January 6, 1919. The war had ended just after the election and now the nation and state could return to peacetime pursuits.

In his message to the legislature, which was, of course, controlled by the Democrats, the Chief Executive spoke of the need to end labor strife and to create a climate of industrial peace. He returned to a suggestion he had made earlier, the creation of a budget system. To show how pioneering Thomas Campbell was in this matter, it must be remembered that the federal government did not adopt such a system until 1921. Other state needs, the lawmakers were told, were the revision of election laws, an anti-usury law and an increase in public health facilities. It is to be remembered that the great influenza epidemic had recently caused many deaths and much suffering. During the election campaign, there was a rumor that Campbell was gravely ill from it and at one point that he had died, all of which were not true.

During this term of office, the members of the armed forces came home from the war and settled back into their civilian lives. There was a brief economic downturn as a result but soon a period of impressive prosperity was at hand. The Governor of Arizona is the ceremonial head of the state and as such the Campbells welcomed the King and Queen of the Belgians who visited the Grand Canyon. Transportation was always important to the state and he dedicated a new airport in Phoenix, rode on the first train to make direct connections from Arizona to San Diego, and urged the construction of new and better roads. It is also always important for the Governor to visit all parts of the state and this Campbell faithfully did.

As the election of 1920 approached, the Governor announced his intention to seek re-election. He had no opposition within his own party and the Democrats' nomination was Milt Simms, a man closely identified with former Governor Hunt. In the midst of the campaign, the Governor charged that the state leasing of land system was unfair and that large areas were given over to a few cattlemen on terms which were well below market value; he also contended that some state lands were being sold under similar terms. When the votes were counted in November, the incumbent had been re-elected by over 5,000 votes, a good margin for a Republican in a Democratic state.

When the new legislature convened in January, 1921, the Governor informed the lawmakers that since the economy was still far from robust, a strict economy in expenditures must be observed. Reforms in financing schools were needed, the highway department needed re-organization, the land code required revision, and attention needed to be paid to water laws. The latter was made necessary by the fact that the states touching the Colorado River were starting to look toward the development of the river and the building of a high dam to generate electricity. In April, 1921, the federal Reclamation Service announced that it would begin studies looking toward a site for the great project.

It was the strong belief of Governor Campbell that Arizona should cooperate with the other states and the federal government in the apportionment of the river's resources. He became President of the League of the Southwest, an organization formed in California to support the dam and its role in the development of the West. The year 1922 was an important one in the story. The federal Colorado River Commission, headed by Secretary of Commerce Herbert Hoover, held several meetings and the Governor of Arizona was supportive of its plans. Campbell was, however, opposed to the original Swing-Johnson Bill which was California's proposal to build the project. Changes were made before the statute became law. In November, 1922, representatives of the states met in the New Mexico capital and drafted the Santa Fe Compact.

The Compact divided the waters of the river between the upper and lower basin states; the states to then apportion the water among themselves. The upper basin states had no

trouble in agreeing, but Arizona, California and Nevada feuded for years. So long as he lived, Thomas E. Campbell believed in the Compact and lived to see his state finally adopt it.

During the campaign of 1922, Campbell acquired the nickname "Traveling Tom." The charge was made by George W. P. Hunt that his adversary spent a good bit of time attending conferences and meetings at state expense. Campbell good naturedly replied that if he was "Traveling Tom," then Hunt was "Galloping George," as that gentleman had also spent time and money in junketeering.

In November, 1922, the Democratic candidate for governor defeated the Republican and thus Tom Campbell left office in January, 1923. By this time in his life, he was relatively well known nationally. In 1920, he had been mentioned for the office of Vice President of the United States but he was not especially interested. If only he had really sought the office, might he have won the nomination of his party? No one can say; but if he had, he would have become President of the United States when Warren G. Harding died in August of 1923. On several occasions Campbell was mentioned as a possible member of the cabinet especially the Office of Secretary of the Interior. He was offered the Ambassadorship to Mexico but as a poor man was unable to accept.

Governor Campbell was very much interested in the problems of Mexico and the Mexican people. He worked to win recognition of the government by the United States during a period of turmoil; he was a close friend of, and a lobbyist for, President Obregon.

Since the Arizonan was unable to serve as Ambassador, President Coolidge in 1926 urged him to take a federal post which would give him a reasonable salary and not cost him extra money. That post was United States Commissioner General for an international exposition to be held in Seville, Spain. The "fair" was held between October, 1928, and January, 1929, and was called a brilliant success. When the Campbells returned home, President Hoover had an assignment for Governor Campbell. He became chairman of the United States Civil Service Commission in June of 1930 and served until 1933 winning the approval of all for his work.

Campbell again sought his former office again in 1936 but was defeated by Judge Stanford. Since his political career was over, Campbell lived a while in Tucson where he managed some agricultural lands in the bankruptcy process and then retired to his home in Phoenix. While leaving the capitol building one afternoon, he suffered a stroke and was rushed to the hospital where he died March 1, 1944. Interment was in the family plot in the Catholic section of Mountain View Cemetery, Prescott. Mrs. Campbell lived with her sons until her death January 30, 1958.

Thomas E. Campbell was an able man who worked hard for the welfare of his state and its people. Honorable, honest and respected by all, he was more than adequate to all tasks which he undertook. He was also a warm, caring, thoroughly likeable man.

## SOURCES

Campbell, Allen, "Republican Politics in Democratic Arizona, Tom Campbell's Career," *Journal of Arizona History*, Summer, 1981

Goff, John S., Thomas E. Campbell, *Arizona Biographical Series*, Cave Creek, 1985

*National Cyclopedia of American Biography*

*Who Was Who in America, 1943—1950*

Young, Herbert V., *Ghosts of Cleopatra Hill*, Jerome, 1964

Governor John C. Phillips
Credit: Arizona Department of Library
Archives and Public Records

# JOHN C. PHILLIPS

## 1929—1931

*Author: Dr. John S.Goff*

Governor Phillips was a modest man with a keen sense of humor and he was often the target of his own jokes. He thought of himself as a homely man, which he was not. For many years he told people that he had once won the "ugly man" contest at the territorial fair —which he really had—and when an opponent accused him of being two faced he immediately replied, "If I had another one, do you think I would wear this one?"

Descended from pioneers who migrated from Wales, John C. Phillips was born on a farm near Vermont, Illinois, November 13, 1870. His father, William Henry Phillips, was a Union Civil War veteran, and his mother was Elizabeth (Wood) Phillips. Raised on the family farm, he was a student in the public schools, and then attended Heading College, Adingdon, Illinois, 1889-1893. Deciding upon the law as a career, he, as so many others had done, studied in the office of a practicing attorney and also took correspondence courses from the Sprague Correspondence School.

On October 24, 1895, he married Minnie Rexroat of Pennington Point, McDonough County, Illinois, a young lady some five years his junior. Both the Phillips and Rexroat families were "Quakers" and upon moving to Arizona, John and Minnie became members of the First Methodist Church. They had three children, a son born in Illinois, and two daughters born in Arizona. Theirs was a happy marriage which lasted nearly a half century, and Mrs. Phillips was a popular First Lady of Arizona. She survived her husband by some thirteen years.

Admitted to the Illinois Bar in 1896, John C. Phillips began his law practice in the town of Vermont but two years later decided to move west. He, his wife and small child arrived in Phoenix on November 17, 1898. It would naturally take a while to be admitted to

the territorial bar and so in the meantime he performed a number of odd jobs including driving a wagon to Vicksburg for the Goldwater family, and buying and selling fruit to the local residents (a fact remembered by the late Governor Sidney P. Osborn.) His first steady job was working as a hod carrier at the capitol then under construction. His wages were $1.75 per day. Phillips saved his money and upon being admitted to the territorial bar, used these savings and a loan from the First National Bank of Arizona for $500 to begin his law practice in 1900. Once a member of the Arizona Bar, he began practice in the city where he would live for the rest of his life.

Under the territorial system, there was an office in each county called the probate judge. Elected by the voters every two years, this official was responsible for the settlement of the estates of deceased persons, but also had such other tasks assigned as being *ex officio* county superintendent of schools. Despite the fact that he had only so recently arrived and being a Republican, in an overwhelmingly Democratic state, Phillips was elected probate judge by the voters of Maricopa County in November, 1900. That time his margin of victory was only 55 votes, but so well regarded was he that he was re-elected five times serving until Arizona became a state in February, 1912.

The office of probate judge was abolished by the new Arizona State Constitution and its duties transferred to the judges of the new superior court. The voters elected the superior court judges in each county and they were the major trial court judges of the state having general, civil and criminal jurisdiction. At the time of admission, Maricopa had only one judge and by virtue of the ballots of the voters he was John C. Phillips. He served until January of 1915.

When Judge Phillips left the bench, he

**Governor Phillips in his Office**
**Credit: Ben D. Cooley, Photographer**

**Governor Phillips by his New Studebaker**

returned to his law practice in Phoenix and his partner was Lysander Cassidy, a boyhood friend from Illinois, who had served in the Arizona Constitutional Convention of 1910. When his partner moved to California, Phillips formed a new law firm with Winfield S. Norviel, later active in water law and the politics of the dividing of the Colorado River waters. By 1919, his son Ralph A. Phillips, had finished law school and so father and son formed a partnership. Although their work was of a general nature, much of it involved probate and estate matters.

In 1918 and 1920, Phillips was elected a member of the state house of representatives and in 1923 was the only Republican serving in the state senate. While serving in the legislature, he learned the ways in which lawmakers worked and this would be of value to him when he was later governor.

There were three candidates seeking the Republican nomination for governor in 1928 but in the September primary John C. Phillips was victorious. He faced Governor George W. P. Hunt in the general election and knew that he faced a difficult campaign since Governor Hunt had served six terms as governor. Herbert Hoover was the Republican nominee for President and he was not terribly popular in Arizona owing to what was seen as his support for California in the battles over the river water. Phillips promised to protect Arizona's interests and was less inclined to cooperate in the building of Hoover Dam than were some members of his party. On November 6, 1928, Phillips defeated Hunt by a vote of 47,829 to 44,553, thus becoming the third state governor of Arizona. While it has been said that he was swept into office by the election of President Herbert Hoover, this does not seem possible since he was the only Republican elected in the Arizona general elections.

The inauguration of Governor Phillips took place at ten o'clock on the morning of January 7, 1929. Chief Justice Lockwood administered the oath of office and some 2,000 people witnessed the ceremony which took place on the balcony at the state capitol.

According to the *Arizona Republican*:

"The simple, straightforward and manly inaugural address of Governor John C. Phillips yesterday bespoke for him the good will of those who heard it. Instead of bristling with platitudes and pledges, the address offered one general pledge of the best that was in the governor in his service of the state, and two specific pledges. The first was that he would be the governor of all the people; therefore his administration would be non-partisan. The other was a pledge of rigid economy as distinct from an ill-advised and mean parsimony."

The new governor spoke for only six minutes, but in that short span of time he mentioned that so many citizens of Arizona had arrived in the state within the last decade, his faith in Arizona, and he pledged rigid economy in governmental expenditures. Remembering that the event took place at a time of unusual prosperity, the "Roaring Twenties" were at their peak, John C. Phillips had some unusual words for the public:

"Our country was founded by people who followed the simple ways of living. These ways of living are safe and sound for us today, and their example in that respect is worthy of our emulation. I am fearful of unusual prosperity, it often leads us to overstep in speculation, and engage in a manner of living beyond the limits of sound business judgment. One of the dangers of prosperity is the belief that it will continue indefinitely, and that hence we are justified in changing our mode of living in keeping with this prosperity; we are apt to draw too heavily upon the future."

The speaker said he was not a pessimist but he wanted to utter a word of caution; in actuality he was predicting the immediate future to an amazing degree. The *Republican* stated further, "Governor Phillips has entered upon his office with the good wishes of a larger majority of the voters of this state than the majority by which he was elected. There is a general hope and belief that his administration will be a successful one. There is no lack of confidence anywhere in his integrity and his sincere desire to be of service to Arizona."

The address closed with an acknowledgement of the power and goodness of Almighty God whose aid was asked in the tasks that should confront him from day to day. A striking expression was that of the governor that the oath of office he had just taken had little to the weight of solemn responsibility that fell upon him with the announcement of his election.

One of the many stories told about him,

which was given wide circulation after his election in 1929 . . . it seems that legislators wanted to increase their salaries and were circulating petitions among the legislators to determine support on the issue. On requesting his support, Governor Phillips is reported to have said, "I can't afford to ask for more money. You know I am the ugliest man in Arizona, and I couldn't get a job at anything else. If my salary was raised, any good lawyer would want this job so where would I be?"

"Governor Phillips has entered upon his office with the good wishes of a larger majority of the voters of this state than the majority by which he was elected. There is a general hope and belief that his administration will be a successful one. There is no lack of confidence anywhere in his integrity and his sincere desire to be of service to Arizona."

The several governors of Arizona have had different approaches to dealing with state legislatures. Whereas Governor Hunt's method had been quite confrontational, Phillips' drew upon his experience as a legislator and sought harmony with the overwhelming Democratic majorities in both the Senate and the House of Representatives. For some years there had been a need for a new state office building but the lawmakers had never been able to agree that Governor Hunt should be involved in the project. In 1929, during the first year of his administration, he appeared before the legislature, requesting appropriations for a $1,000,000 construction program of public works, including the erection of the State Building on the corner of 17th Avenue and Adams Street in the capitol. The legislature entrusted Governor Phillips with the necessary appropriations to complete these programs, which had been denied the previous Governor. Despite the fact that over $1,000,000 was spent in public works projects, one of the most ambitious programs ever undertaken by the state, no hint of misapplication of funds was ever raised and he was able to return over $100,000 to the state treasury of the money appropriated for this purpose. His friends gave him the nickname of "Honest John." In reality, it was a compliment to the simplicity of his life and the quality of his character. A tribute to his honesty was made at the dedication of Coolidge Dam by former President Calvin Coolidge in speaking to the residents of Arizona when he said of Governor

Phillips, "You are safe in the hands of Governor Phillips. He is a modest gentleman and from that modesty comes candor. He is a worthy, honest, conscientious, upright, public servant. If I were paying money into a treasury, I would rejoice in having it expended under his direction."

John C. Phillips was a life-long fisherman and one of his interests as chief executive was securing enactment of a bill which created the fish and game department. Some years later when he passed his seventieth birthday, he was presented with an honorary lifetime hunting and fishing license for his efforts. Another bill which had the strong support of the Governor was the law to make it illegal to destroy or mutilate desert plants. The lawmakers went on record as asking the federal government to construct and maintain roads in the national forests and on Indian lands and this, too, met with the Governor's approval.

A major problem inherited by the Phillips' administration was that of the distribution of the Colorado River waters as well as the electrical power generated by any such project. The legislature created a Colorado River Commission and the Governor worked well with it. In December, 1928, the Congress passed the Swing-Johnson proposal which authorized the building of Boulder Dam. Work was started on July 7, 1930. Arizona fought the matter in the courts while at the same time attempting to resolve the issue of dividing the waters among the lower basin states. Governor Phillips urged that Arizona, California, and Nevada reach a tri-state river pact. Arizona made a proposal regarding amounts of water each state would be allotted but California rejected it and there was deadlock. One very touchy issue was California's insistence that the waters of the Gila River be considered, something opposed by the Arizona governor.

As the Governor noted in his inaugural address, the population of Arizona had grown substantially in the last decade. The census of 1930 would reveal there were more than 435,000 people in the state; the capital city reached a size of 70,000. A new form of transportation was arriving on the scene— Globe-Miami, Kingman, Chandler, Casa Grande and Florence all opened airports in 1929 and 1930. On June 2, 1930, a Phoenix radio station became the first in the state to join

**(left to right) Mrs. Calvin Coolidge, Mrs. Minnie Phillips, President Calvin Coolidge, and Governor John Phillips**

**Governor Phillips Enjoying his Favorite Pastime—Fishing**

a national broadcasting network and thus bring the outside world to the Southwest. In February, 1929, the new multi-million dollar Arizona Biltmore opened. All of these events and conditions promised a good future.

When the stock market crashed in October, 1929, few in Arizona seemed to notice. The next month Governor Phillips telegraphed President Hoover that the state's building program for the coming year would be the greatest in history. The following month of January was proclaimed "Prosperity Month" by the Governor, but by April the word depression was starting to appear in Arizona newspapers. Banks began to fail. In October the Chief Executive announced a plan to register the unemployed so as to help them find jobs. By the end of the year, Phillips wanted to erect a tent city using national guard equipment but the attorney general ruled against it.

Governor Phillips maintained a budget balance for both 1929 and 1930. Also, at the completion of his administration, he left over $11,000 to the incoming governor for the operation of his office. During the first year of his administration, he appeared before the legislature, which was Democratic controlled, requesting appropriation for a $1,000,000 construction program of public works, including the erection of the State Building on the corner of 17th Avenue and Adams Street in the capitol. The legislature entrusted Governor Phillips with the appropriations for large building programs which had been denied the previous Governor. Despite the fact that over $1,000,000 was spent in public works projects, one of the most ambitious programs ever undertaken by the state, no hint of misapplication of funds was ever raised and he was able to return over $100,000 to the state treasury of the money appropriated for this purpose.

Governor Phillips kept his promise to the voters to maintain a rigid economy in hard times by showing a balanced budget for both 1929 and 1930. He was so adamant about a balanced budget he is reputed to have refused to afford it at this time. While he was only left $1 by the previous governor for the operation of his office, at the completion of administration, he left over $11,000 to the incoming governor for this purpose. During his administration, taxes were lower than they

had previously been, despite the fact that a law had just been enacted granting exemptions to widows and ex-servicemen on property, having a total valuation of $2 million.

Prior to his taking office, the law of the state allowed for the appointment of a game warden to supervise and enforce the game and fish laws of the state, which appointment in many instances, had been made as a reward for party services rendered, rather than the man appointed who was most qualified. Governor Phillips was an enthusiastic sportsman particularly interested in hunting and fishing and during his administration, a law was enacted by legislature establishing a fish and game commission, and the first commissioners to be appointed were selected by him. In 1930, Zane Grey, the famous author, requested permission to take several friends bear hunting on the Mogollon Rim . . . out of season permission was denied by his appointee, Lee Bayless. In a subsequent conversation with Governor Phillips by Zane Grey, Governor Phillips backed up the decision by Lee Bayless and Zane Grey was so enraged that he left Arizona never to return again.

The present method of operating the Arizona Game and Fish Commission is a continuation of the program he helped to implement during his administration. Some years later when he passed his seventieth birthday he was presented with an honorary lifetime hunting and fishing license for his efforts.

In the Republican primary of 1930, Governor Phillips was renominated without opposition. His Democratic opponent was George W. P. Hunt. The Governor opened his re-election campaign in Prescott on the evening of October 1, having spoken informally earlier in the day in Wickenburg. In the succeeding weeks he canvassed the state and defended his stewardship. The year was not a good one for Republicans in general but Phillips came close to being re-elected, a testament to his personal popularity. The final returns showed vote totals of 48,875 to 46,231. In January, 1931, "Honest John" Phillips retired to private life.

The depression had arrived and inspite of his success and popularity as the governor, he was defeated in the election of 1930 by a very narrow margin by ex-Governor Hunt. This was his first defeat in an election for public office.

He had an outstanding career as governor. He was the only chief executive who went through his term without calling a special session of the legislature. Governor Phillips' administration was marked by: (1) Harmony with the legislature and state government officials; (2) A progressive program of public works; including the erection of the Arizona State Building at 17th Avenue and Adams Street; (3) A balanced budget in "hard times"; (4) The creation of the Game and Fish Commission; and (5) Lower taxes.

After retiring from politics the second time, he returned to the practice of law with the firm Phillips, Holzworth, and Phillips, which later became Phillips, Holzworth, Phillips and Jones. The former governor practiced law until the late 30s when he began to think of retirement and spent less time with the law and more with his beloved fishing.

John Phillips was an inveterate fisherman, frequently taking trips to California and the Oregon coast to fish for salmon and trout. During his later years, he took many trips to Florida to try his hand fishing for marlin. He was a yearly visitor to the "White Mountains" and owned a cabin at Mormon Lake, where he was a "regular," along with Len and Paul Thornburg and R. C. Railey, fishing around the banks of Lake Mary and Mormon Lake. He had had a heart problem during a fishing expedition to the Klamath River in 1941 and had been warned to slow down. In May, 1943, he spent some time in Greer fishing with several members of the Becker family and then to Mormon Lake and Lake Mary. While fishing with the Thornbergs at Lake Mary, he suffered a heart attack and died in a Flagstaff hospital on June 25, 1943. Governor Osborn who had known him ever since he came to Phoenix eulogized him as "one of the kindest and most sincere men I have ever known." After lying in state in the capitol, he was entombed in the mausoleum of Greenwood Memorial Park, Phoenix.

## SOURCES

*National Cyclopedia of American Biography*
*Arizona Republic*, June 26, 1943
*Who Was Who in America*, 1943-1950
Additional information provided by:
    Mrs. Barbara Pierce
    Mr. John P. Phillips

Mr. John M. Robbins
Mr. Joseph S. Robbins, Jr.

Governor Benjamin B. Moeur
Credit: Arizona Department of Library
Archives and Public Records

# DR. BENJAMIN B. MOEUR

## 1933—1937

*Author: Richard E. Lynch*

Benjamin Baker Moeur, country doctor, businessman, community leader, and Arizona's Great Depression governor, entered this world on December 22, 1869, in Decherd, Tennessee, a small community about seventy miles southeast of Nashville. Earlier that year the first transcontinental railroad had been completed at Promontory, Utah. Americans by the score were pulling up stakes and heading west with the railroads. At the age of four, this son of a Parisian-born French father, Dr. John B. Moeur, and a pioneer-family Tennessee mother, Esther Kelly Knight, found himself in the flow of the westward migration heading for Texas.

Young Ben Moeur grew up along the south Texas plain, north of the Rio Grande Valley, along the corridor that U. S. Highway 90 now travels between Del Rio and San Antonio. His father set up his medical practice there, his aunt and uncle began ranching in the area, and his father, too, soon entered the cattle business and put Ben aboard the hurricane deck of a Texas cow pony. Between the ages of six and twenty B. B. Moeur was one of the original cowboys. He read when he could, completed grade school and high school, but mostly punched cows.

In his late teens Ben Moeur worked for a cattleman named Anderson, who happened one day by the cow camp where the young Tennesseean was working and proudly showed his hired hands a new photograph of his daughter. Young Ben was smitten and allowed as how he maybe would like to marry that girl. Anderson replied that she would never marry a cowboy. According to family legend it was then that Benjamin B. Moeur decided to follow in the footsteps of his grandfather and become a doctor.

In 1889, at the age of twenty, the former cowboy entered the Arkansas Industrial University at Little Rock, later the University of Arkansas, to pursue his medical education. Some time later, in the midst of his studies, he returned to Texas to meet the object of his dreams on the occasion of her graduation from high school. Honor Glint Anderson, the future first lady of Arizona, obviously approved of this romantic and industrious suitor who worshipped from afar, for she decided to teach school and wait two years while he finished medical school. Young Ben graduated with high honors, receiving a gold medal for the highest average in his class, and then went on to Rush Medical College in Chicago for postgraduate training. In 1896, he returned to Texas, married Honor Anderson, and, taking the advice of his older brother, William, moved to Arizona.

Tombstone, fabled frontier home of Wyatt Earp, Doc Holliday and Big-Nosed Kate, was the first stop for the newlyweds, and there the new doctor hung out his first shingle. Not too long thereafter, however, the Moeurs moved on to Bisbee where he contracted to serve as relief physician for the Copper Queen Hospital. It seemed the physician in charge needed a rest on the Continent. Unfortunately, Honor Moeur suffered from asthma, and the sulphur smoke from the smelter stacks irritated her lungs more than she could stand. She soon fled to Tempe to stay with her brother-in-law and his wife, the William A. Moeurs, while her husband fulfilled his contract.

When B. B. Moeur arrived in Tempe he found his wife much improved. They decided they liked the community that brother Will had picked. They were determined to set up a practice again and put down roots. The young doctor soon purchased the home they were renting on the northwest corner of Seventh and Myrtle, and they never moved again. The home still stands, much enlarged over the years

**Governor Benjamin B. Moeur**
**Credit: Arizona Department of Library**
**Archives and Public Records**

**Benjamin B. Moeur**
**Circa 1895**
**Credit: Arizona Department of Library**
**Archives and Public Records**

to hold the Moeur's growing family, but now neglected with no current occupant to keep it up to the standards it possessed when it housed Arizona's governor. In this home Dr. Moeur and his wife had four children: John Kelly was born in Tempe in 1897, Vyvyan Bernice in 1898, Jessie Belle in 1901 and Benjamin Baker, Jr. in 1903.

In the years that accompanied the formation of his family, Doc Moeur became one of the busiest and best known horse and buggy doctors of the Salt River Valley. He delivered most of Tempe's babies and was much called upon by the outlying farms, ranches and small hamlets. He had stables and a red barn to care for his horses, and even after many of the valley's farm-to-market roads had been paved the doctor acquired a Franklin automobile, he kept a horse and buggy for the late night excursions into the rutted backroad hinterlands.

In the years before the construction of Theodore Roosevelt Dam, the Doc had many harrowing experiences as he forded the flowing Salt to reach an expectant mother or tend to a deathly ill patient. Quicksand and high water sucked at his wheels and threatened to dump him in the river. Later the damsite served as a makeshift bridge. The Doc was hauled across the canyon in a construction cable bucket to attend to a sick woman on the other side. Babies, however, were his stock-in-trade, and over the years Doc Moeur delivered thousands of them. After Moeur's entry into the political arena, the great humorist Will Rogers once remarked that all those babies grew up and elected him governor.

As the Gay Nineties made way for the twentieth century, the Salt River Valley began to enjoy the growth made possible by the construction of Roosevelt Dam, B. B. Moeur became a leading citizen and businessman in Tempe. An avid southern Democrat, Moeur actively participated in precinct, in county and in state Democratic party circles. He ran a drugstore for several years before his burgeoning medical practice made it impossible to do both, served as president of the South-side Electric Light and Gas Company, and headed the Moeur-Pafford Company, a ranching and cattle-raising operation. His years of living the cowboy's life had made cattle raising a part of his blood, and he had an interest in several ranches in the valley for many years.

Fundamentally interested in education, Doc served for years on the Board of Education for the Normal School at Tempe, today's Arizona State University, and during twelve of those years he acted as secretary of the board. In addition, he provided free medical care to the students, and many of them just came to him when they needed to talk. His interest in education and his prominence in Democratic party circles won him a seat in the constitutional convention and a hand in writing Arizona's state constitution in 1910, serving as chairman of the education committee and as a member of the committees on suffrage and elections, and counties and municipalities.

As chairman of the education committee, Moeur soon called on Dr. Arthur J. Matthews, president of the Territorial Normal School, with a request. He asked Matthews to draft the educational provisions of the new constitution and to have the draft ready in a week. Matthews dropped everything and accomplished the job on schedule, drawing heavily upon existing Arizona school law, those of California and Maryland, and the advice of the Teachers' Association of Arizona. He purposely left out all references to school segregation, and, much to Moeur's credit, the chairman placed the draft before his colleagues without change and saw it through his committee with only minor verbal changes. Ardent segregationists were furious, and perhaps the most bitter floor fight of the convention ensued splitting the delegates down the middle, but thanks to Dr. Matthews and Dr. Moeur, segregation did not become part of Arizona's constitution.

During the First World War the forty-eight-year-old doctor showed his community spirit and patriotism by forgiving the medical debts of boys who went off to fight and delivering free medical care to their families at home. He also later remarked that he never charged a widow or a preacher for his professional services. Toward the end of the war, Moeur watched his brother Will, then Arizona State Land Commissioner, throw his hat in the Democratic primary for the governor's race. After a time, Will withdrew under heavy political pressure, but nevertheless he pointed the way for his younger brother in 1932. Ben had followed Will to Arizona, and he seemed to follow in those footsteps again as

**(left to right) Unknown, Eddie Cantor, Governor Benjamin B. Moeur**
**Arizona Biltmore Hotel**
**Credit: Arizona Department of Library**
**Archives and Public Records**

**(seated front, left) Mrs. Benjamin Moeur, Governor Moeur
and prominent Arizonans
Credit: Arizona Department of Library
Archives and Public Records**

the nation sank deeper into the Great Depression.

What he perceived as soaring taxes, reckless government spending and a need for change in state government provoked B. B. Moeur into the Democratic primary against the venerable old campaigner and seven-times governor George W. P. Hunt. Hunt was the incumbent with a seemingly unbeatable lock on the Democratic nomination, but the country and the state were in trouble. Dr. Moeur stumped the state literally shouting for economy in government and lower state property taxes. When the votes were counted, Hunt had lost his first primary ever by a margin of almost 5,000 votes. Moeur went on to easily win the governor's chair over Republican J. C. Kinney with a plurality of 33,000 votes and at a campaign cost of only $75.80.

Less than an hour after the convening of the legislature, while hundreds of Arizona's unemployed milled about the capitol carrying signs, Governor Moeur stepped to the podium of the House of Representatives amid "prolonged" applause and after a few words of greeting asked the indulgence of the legislators in having his message read by his executive secretary Herbert Hotchkiss. Received in relative silence, the governor's message called for strict economies and a massive reorganization of state government. The new governor had inherited a 7 1/2 million dollar shortfall in revenues, 19,000 Arizonans on the relief rolls, 28,000 applicants for state jobs, and state warrants selling at a 20 percent discount because there was not enough money in the treasury to redeem them. Many banks had already failed and soon would come the federal bank holiday in March, 1933. In the first ever broadcast of the governor's message to the legislature he called for the abolition of the state highway commission, the consolidation of nine other boards and commissions into just three, a twenty percent cut in salaries and wages for all state employees, twenty percent budget cuts for the state's three schools of higher education, and a $500,000 reduction in appropriations for elementary schools. The governor had a critically ill patient on his hands, and a dire situation called for drastic measures.

Over the next two years Governor Moeur instituted the state's first sales tax, income tax and luxury tax. With the cooperation of the legislature he succeeded in reducing the general property tax rate by twenty-seven percent while at the same time raising revenues. The governor also reduced state expenditures to the tune of $4,500,000. He worked with the federal government to bring $22,500,000 in New Deal programs to Arizona, and at the end of his first term the state was virtually on a cash basis with state warrants selling at full value.

In spite of all the strong medicine prescribed by the Doc during his first term and the removal of his patient from the economic critical list, he is perhaps best remembered for his declaration of martial law to protect the state's interest in the Colorado River from the omnivorous water appetite of the City of Los Angeles. The dispute with the Metropolitan Water District of Los Angeles and the Bureau of Reclamation arose when the District commissioned the Bureau to build Parker Dam in exchange for the water to be impounded behind it. In trying to forestall the project until an agreement could be reached safeguarding Arizona's rights to the river, Governor Moeur argued that because Congress had not authorized the construction of Parker Dam, the Bureau of Reclamation had no right to set foot on Arizona soil to build the dam, and he pledged to stop the trespass.

On March 9, 1934, Governor Moeur dispatched a small contingent of Arizona national guardsmen to Parker to act as observers and to alert the governor should reclamation crews venture toward Arizona's shore. To reconnoiter the damsite and to later transport additional men and material to a campsite near the mouth of the Bill Williams River, Nellie T. Bush, a community leader in Parker, hotel owner, ferryboat operator and loyal Democratic member of the Arizona House of Representative, offered the use of two of her ferryboats. The press promptly dubbed the *Julia B* and the *Nellie T* the Arizona Navy and made Mrs. Bush Chief Boatswain's Mate. The national press and especially the *Los Angeles Times* had a field day making fun of the Colorado River Expeditionary Force and the Arizona Navy, but it did not seem to bother Moeur who enjoyed being a character and playing to the crowd. To the press he quipped, "We may get licked, but we'll go down fighting." He bided his time until he received word in November that construction crews had

begun to assemble a trestle bridge headed for Arizona.

Having informed President Franklin D. Roosevelt and Secretary of the Interior Harold Ickes of his intention, Governor Moeur declared martial law over the Arizona side of the Parker damsite. He then dispatched an eighteen-truck convoy containing forty infantrymen from Phoenix and twenty machine gunners from Prescott to "repel the threatened invasion of sovereignty" of Arizona. Three days later an embarrassed Secretary Ickes ordered a halt in construction until the courts could decide the issues in dispute. It was the outcome which Governor Moeur had worked for from the beginning. He had won the first battle, and the second when the United States Supreme Court ruled in Arizona's favor stating that Parker was technically illegal since Congress had not in fact authorized it. The big battle was lost, however, when four months later California's delegation succeeded in securing congressional approval for Parker without so much as a comma concerning Arizona's rights to the river. Nevertheless, Governor Moeur symbolically left his martial law decree in effect for the remainder of his two terms in office.

In the Fall of 1934, B. B. Moeur faced George W. P. Hunt once again in the Democratic primary with the addition of a strong third candidate and New Deal Democrat, Judge Rawghlie C. Stanford. For the first time in his political career, Hunt ran third as Moeur edged Stanford by 5,000 votes for the nomination. In the general election Governor Moeur faced the Republican's "seasoned-campaigner" Thomas Maddock and won by 22,000 votes.

The elation of a campaign victory and plans for a second term were put on hold in early December, 1934 when the Governor's elder son, John Kelly Moeur, entered St. Joseph's Hospital in Phoenix. The younger Moeur had also become a doctor and had assumed part of his father's practice, but he was not well and an automobile accident the previous March had shocked an already weakened constitution. Dr. John, as he was known, passed away at only 37 years of age. It has been said by the family that Doc Moeur had entered politics as a salve against the hurt he felt at not being able to help his son regain his health. Greatly saddened, the Governor

again turned to his official duties.

During his second term in office, Governor Moeur continued to work for the homeless and unemployed while occasionally stepping outside his official capacity to perform his medical duties free of charge. He persuaded the legislature to appropriate funds to send a representative to Washington to solicit federal relief dollars for Arizona's needy. For a Jeffersonian Democrat this was a difficult course to follow, but it is a measure of the man that he did.

Contrary to earlier campaign promises but with the encouragement of friends and political associates, Governor Moeur threw his hat in the Democratic primary for the third time in 1936, only to be defeated by Judge Stanford. Governor Moeur has been portrayed as a gruff, gritty, profane man who could swear for fifteen minutes and not repeat himself. It has also been said his cigar-smoking, blunt-speaking exterior was just a facade and that he had a heart of gold. It should now be added that he was a wise statesman and a gentleman, for at the end of his career, Governor Moeur was the first of Arizona's governors to welcome his successor to his new office, to be present at the swearing in of his successor and to invite the new governor to place his department heads in their new offices beside his own people before the inauguration to insure a smooth transition.

Only some three months after he left office, Dr. Benjamin Moeur was dead. A heart ailment which had plagued him during his terms of office and which had become particularly acute during the campaigning of 1936, took him on March 16, 1937. He had tended to an ill patient who needed all of his attention, and he did not take the time to attend to himself. B. B. Moeur will be remembered with many humorous anecdotes. He will be remembered with rancor and with respect. Let him also be remembered as one who cared deeply for his fellow citizens and for his state.

## SOURCES

"About Arizona Politics, Medical Problems",
    *Tempo*, April 2, 1976, p. 12
Conners, Jo, *Who's Who in Arizona,*
    Arizona Daily Star, Tucson, Arizona,
    1913
Finch, Jessie Belle Moeur, "Father-Doctor-

Governor Recalled," *Tempo,* March
26, 1976, p. 2

Goff, John S. *George W. P. Hunt and His
Arizona,* Socio Technical Publications,
Pasadena, California, 1973

Griggs, Anna Mae, "Arizona Governor,"
*Arizona Highways,* 1933, p. 1-2

Hopkins, Ernest J., and Alfred Thomas,
Jr., *The Arizona State University
Story,* Southwest Publishing
Company, Phoenix, Arizona, 1960

McClintock, James H., *Arizona,* S. J. Clarke
Publishing Company, Chicago,
Illinois, 1916

Moeur Biographical File, State Library,
Arizona Department of Library,
Archives and Public Records, State
Capitol, Phoenix, Arizona

O'Connor, Jack, *Horse and Buggy West,*
Alfred A. Knopf, New York, 1969

Peplow, Edward H., Jr., *History of Arizona,*
Lewis Publishing Company, New
York, 1958

Reisner, Marc, *Cadillac Desert,* Viking
Penguin, New York, 1986

Sloan, Richard E., and Ward R. Adams,
*History of Arizona,* Record
Publishing Company, Phoenix,
Arizona, 1930

Trimble, Marshall, *Arizona,* Doubleday and
Company, Garden City, New York,
1977

"Who the Constitution Makers Were," *Arizona*
Vol. 1, 1910, p.15

**Governor Rawghlie C. Stanford**
**Credit: Arizona Department of Library**
**Archives and Public Records**

# RAWGHLIE C. STANFORD

## 1937—1939

*Author: Christine N. Marin*

The Great Depression which began in 1929 brought difficult economic changes to Arizona, and the Republican Party was blamed for the state's financial problems. The Democrats, on the other hand, controlled the legislature and most political offices in the state and were viewed as having the solutions to pull Arizona out of its economic slump. Rawghlie Clement Stanford was named to head their ticket in the 1936 campaign. He eased into a quick victory, riding high on the coat-tails of President Franklin Delano Roosevelt's successful and much-needed 1933 New Deal program, which also benefitted the state of Arizona.

The Roosevelt Administration introduced new philosophies and concepts of public finance experimentism to Arizona through the implementation of federal programs such as the Federal Emergency Relief Administration (FERA), the Civilian Conservation Corps (CCC), and the Works Progress Administration (WPA). The unemployed were put to work throughout the state to construct and to improve sanitation and water systems, to build roads and dig irrigation systems, and to develop local parks and community neighborhoods. By the time Rawghlie C. Stanford became the state's fifth governor in 1937, jobs were created and the state was on its road to some sort of economic recovery, thanks to the Democratic party.

Rawghlie Clement Stanford was born on August 2, 1878, in Buffalo Gap, Texas, but his family came to Arizona in 1881 by way of covered wagon. He grew up on the family's farm, which occupied 80 acres on the south side of McDowell Road, just four miles east of Phoenix. He attended Creighton Schools, and later studied one year at the Tempe Normal School. In 1894, he graduated from Lamson Business College. As a youth, Stanford easily adapted to a farm life, and became quite good at taking care of farm animals, especially horses. He used his equestrian skills to earn money as a bronco rider in various rodeos throughout the state. But young Stanford sought more adventure. He found it when he enlisted in the Army. Stanford served almost two years in the Philippine Islands in the Spanish-American War, and held the rank of a sergeant when he was discharged in 1901.

After military service, Stanford decided to pursue a career in law and studied under two capable and respected judges, Fred Sutter, of Bisbee, and Judge Armstrong, of Phoenix. Admitted to the Arizona State Bar in 1907, the same year he married Ruth Butchell, also of Buffalo Gap, Texas, Stanford practiced law in Cochise County for two years before he moved to Phoenix, where he practiced law for eight more years.

In 1914, Stanford was elected to the office of judge of Maricopa County Superior Court, and served two terms, from 1915 to 1918, and also during 1919 to 1922. Stanford's most important and controversial ruling occurred in 1916-1917. At issue was the governorship for the state of Arizona. George Wiley Paul Hunt was not re-elected to the office, according to the official ballot counts, and was defeated by Thomas E. Campbell. Hunt challenged the ballot count, and refused to accept the outcome of the election. He even refused to vacate his state office at the Capitol. The dispute over who really was the governor of Arizona had to be determined in a court of law. Judge Rawghlie Stanford ruled that Campbell won the election, but the Arizona Supreme Court gave the election to Hunt.

Stanford's reputation as a fair, sensitive, and erudite judge made him a formidable candidate for a high political office.

**Governor Rawghlie C. Stanford**
**Credit: The Phoenix Newspapers**

Democrats knew of his fine reputation and of his public appeal. Stanford, on the other hand, was genuinely interested in aiding his community, his political party, and his state.

In 1920, he tested those political waters. He sought, but lost, the Democratic nomination for the United States Senate. Stanford remained undaunted and posed a challenge to Governor Benjamin B. Moeur in the primary of 1934 for the gubernatorial nomination. He lost that primary race, but his political career would soon be revived and given a new challenge during the remaining Depression years.

Under the Republican party, Arizona was not successful in recovering totally from the Great Depression. Political opportunists were smart enough to know that the governorship could easily go to a Democrat in the next election, since F. D. R.'s popularity and personality virtually guaranteed a new governor for the state. And Rawghlie C. Stanford became that governor.

Stanford's initial concern as he took office in 1937 related to various issues. He actively worked on water reclamation projects which would divert water from the Colorado River into Central Arizona above the Boulder Dam. Stanford also became concerned with larger issues such as proper water usage, control, and reclamation projects. He knew that Arizona's water policies and water legislation would easily capture the attention of President Roosevelt who urged the conservation of natural resources by encouraging the development of watershed programs. Stanford supported his party's philosophy of flood control and the preservation of the nation's water supply.

While Stanford tended to state affairs at the federal level, he constantly struggled to maintain an economic balance at home. The effect of the Depression on the citizens of the state served to remind him that all was not completely well for those unfortunates who remained unemployed, hungry, and also dispossessed.

His own personal friends and acquaintances and his political supporters constantly asked and begged him for economic and political favors; i.e., jobs, political appointments, and other financial considerations. His door was always open to those who sought his favors, his free advice, and his kind and generous attention. At times, his critics demanded that he spend less time trying to solve everyone else's problems, and stick to the problems at home which needed his precious time. Poor Stanford could not please everyone, and he could please no one.

The political press criticized him when he favored his so-called friends, and they hounded him for neglecting the needs of the poor, who were still being fed from open and public soup kitchens. Homeless families with children were even camping out on the lawn of the governor's home.

Stanford anguished over his inability to bring economic prosperity to the average citizen and struggled with his own conscience over how to deal with controversy over his political decisions. He especially felt saddened that he could not give jobs to those in the most desperate need of work, and he disliked having to reject his friends' pleas for economic assistance.

Soon, Rawghlie Stanford found his political duties and responsibilities too distasteful. He tired of the give-and-take of manipulative and political games so inherent in the life of a politician.

In August, 1937, Stanford announced that he would not run for another term as governor. He preferred the orderly and predictable life of a judge, and he yearned to return to a judicial role. He was soon elected to the State Supreme Court for two terms, 1943-1955.

Rawleigh Clement Stanford served only one term as governor of the state of Arizona. But as a public official who found the responsibilities of the office too demanding, Stanford did enable the state to successfully ease out of the grips of the Great Depression and guided it in to a new sense of growth and change. He remained a forceful figure in maintaining and enforcing judicial and legal matters. Even though the state's economic stability was slightly improving when he left office and new administrative agencies were making solid gains and prosperous decisions, Stanford's term in office was somewhat disappointing. His sense of dignity and kindness for others served him well as a judge throughout his life as a public servant but spelled his downfall from any further ambitions. Stanford died in Phoenix at the age of 85 on December 15, 1963.

## SOURCES

*Arizona Biographical Dictionary,* Cave Creek,
Arizona: Black Mountain Press, 1983
*Arizona Republic,* August 19, 1937
*Dunbar's Weekly*, December 28, 1934
Goff, John S., *American Biographical
Encyclopedia.*, Volume 5, Phoenix,
Arizona, Paul W. Pollock Publisher,
1981
*Men and Women of Arizona: Past and Present.*
Phoenix: Pioneer Publishing Co., 1940
Shadegg, Stephen C., *Arizona Politics:  The
Struggle To End One-party Rule*,
Tempe, Arizona State University, 1986
Statement of Governor R. C. Stanford of
Arizona To Boulder Dam Power
Conference, Called by Honorable
Harold L. Ickes, Secretary of Interior at
Washington, D.C., April 16, 1937

57

**Governor Robert T. Jones**
**Credit: Arizona Department of Library**
**Archives and Public Records**

# ROBERT T. JONES

## 1939—1941

*Author: Anna Laura Bennington*

Robert Taylor Jones, a southern gentleman who never lost his southern accent, came to Arizona in 1909 from Tennessee. He was born in the town of Rutledge, February 8, 1884, and named after a popular political figure. R. T. Jones was a civil engineer when he moved to Arizona. He became a civil engineer the hard way—he earned it by working on construction projects in Mexico and on the Panama Canal.

On December 23, 1911, he married Elon Marion Armstrong in Dudleyville, Arizona. They had two children, Kathryn and Albert. History reveals R. T. Jones served in the Spanish-American War.

Switching to business from engineering, Jones had the first drug store in Superior, Arizona. While governor he owned drug stores in Phoenix and Tucson. He later owned a western store in Phoenix and raised cattle. His political background included serving three terms in the Arizona Senate, representing Pinal County and later Maricopa County, and serving as president of the senate during his second term. The period of time served in the senate was prior to his election as governor—from 1931-1935. During his second term, he was president of the Senate.

A druggist for 20 years himself, he came from a family of druggists. Among the family relics was a 150-year-old pharmacopeia. One of the Jones ancestors was a chemist who manufactured the powder that helped win the battle of New Orleans. He opened a drug store in Tucson at Scott and Congress in the Summer of 1933 which had a soda fountain, light lunches, and a full line of all drugs and accessories. In 1938 the leading Democratic candidate for governor, M. C. Zander, was killed in an airplane crash while campaigning. Jones replaced him on the ballot. He served as governor from 1939-1940 and ran for a second term in 1940, announcing his candidacy in May, 1940. He lost in the primary to Sidney P. Osborn. His inaugural speech can be listened to which reveals he believed . . . "in increased cooperation between city, county, and state governments to effect greater economies and efficiency for the lasting benefit of every resident of Arizona."

In Arizona at that time, the governor's hand was weakened because he could not act as spokesman for the executive branch in his dealings with the legislature. The governor's position could be strengthened if he were given greater appointive and supervisory authority.

Another hindrance to gubernatorial leadership in Arizona is the unsophisticated nature of political attitudes and practices, Jones felt.

The Arizona Constitution provides the governor with two positive tools to influence legislation: the power to recommend and the power to call special sessions of the legislature.

The veto is a power of the Governor—but remains a negative tool as the governor does not act but rather reacts when exercising the veto.

Keeping in mind the foregoing limitations of the Governor of Arizona and the time frame of 1939-1940, a review of his inaugural address given January 11, 1939, outlines his accomplishments. His message was brief, clear, and reasonable with just enough controversial proposals to arouse enlightening and needed debate which did not ask for a single punitive measure against business and industry. He started his administration with good feelings and a spirit of cooperation.

Governor Jones inherited one of the highest tax rates in the history of the state. Quoting him, ". . . however, by careful economies and good management I am proud

**Governor and Mrs. Robert Jones**
**Credit: Arizona Department of Library**
**Archives and Public Records**

to say that we were able to reduce the tax rate by one-third at the end of my first year in office."

Three state institutions raised their levels of operations and management. New buildings were constructed at a minimum cost to the taxpayers.

Cooperation with the United States Public Health Service was mentioned in his message to the legislature in 1939, and in reviewing the accomplishments, new buildings were constructed and new equipment was installed. The state hospital director was among his 32 appointments made and confirmed by the Senate. A total of 1,063 patients were returned to society and their homes. Arizona become the first state in the union to have a state-wide food stamp plan during Governor Jones' term.

The invasion of Europe by Hitler was on the horizon as Jones took office. Arizona and the nation were talking about the specter of World War II. Fort Huachuca was enlarged and improved with federal funds. Other federal funds brought into the state during his term of office included funds for the highway from Ajo to the Mexican border. Thousand of tourists would take advantage of this highway.

Through the efforts of the people in Arizona and the representatives in Washington, Arizona became a recipient of the Boulder Dam Power—$300,000 each year for 50 years.

Selling Arizona through the promotion of tourism was one of the goals Governor Jones listed in his address to the legislatures; the state was successful! The motion picture industry spent millions of dollars in the state during 1939-1940.

The mines of the state operated at full capacity. An effort of the people of the state working and fighting to continue the four cent excise tax on copper proved to be successful. Quoting Governor Jones, "If this excise tax had been eliminated, every large copper producer in the state would have been forced to suspend operations and thousands of men and women would have been thrown out of work."

The composition of the legislature during Governor Jones' term of office was 1 (one) Republican and 51 (fifty one) Democrats in the house of representatives, and 19 (nineteen) Democrats in the senate with 0 (zero) Republicans. The state was referred to as a "one" party state! Governor Jones called one special session of the legislature during his two years; he vetoed five (5) bills after adjournment.

Governor Jones made trips to Washington and lobbied for old age pensions and the statewide food stamp program. In his message to the legislature in 1939, he stated "Every fair minded citizen will recognize the obligation we owe to those who are old and needy, those who are crippled and blind, and to those, who through no fault of their own, are unemployed."

The Pioneers' Home, despite a 20 percent increase in population, was run so efficiently it turned back a substantial part of its yearly appropriation to the general fund. An appropriation from the Federal Government was obtained to construct new buildings for the Fort Grant Institution. The labor was furnished by WPA and replaced barracks which had been built in 1870.

He worked with the citizens of Bisbee to supply Ft. Huachuca with water. Other efforts toward World War II included the Arizona National Guard on a wartime footing—armed with automatic rifles.

After his unsuccessful bid in the primary election of 1940, Jones returned to private business. For two years he was head of the Office of Price Stabilization in Phoenix.

He died in Phoenix, Arizona, after complications arising from abdominal surgery on June 11, 1958.

SOURCES

*Arizona Daily Star*

Dickinson, Joel Ray, *Office and Powers of the Governor of Arizona*, 1966

Historical Library—Tucson

Morey, Roy D., *Politics and Legislation: The Office of the Governor of Arizona*, 1964

*Phoenix Daily Gazette*

Research—State Capitol Building, Phoenix

*Tucson Citizen*

Tucson Public Library

University of Arizona Library—Tucson
    Special Collections, The University of Arizona

*Young Democrat*

**Governor Sidney P. Osborn**
**Credit: Arizona Department of Library**
**Archives and Public Records**

# SIDNEY P. OSBORN

## 1941—1948

*Author: Margaret Finnerty*

More than any other Arizona Governor, Sidney Osborn lived his entire life enmeshed in the state's history. From pioneer days through the dawn of the atomic era, he was either an observer or a participant, and often both. He was passionately dedicated to serving Arizona. "Only death or the people of Arizona," he promised, "will remove me from office." The people never did.

The Osborn family had been in Arizona years before the Salt River Valley was a place to visit. Osborn's grandparents, John and Perlina Osborn, arrived in Prescott, then the territorial capital, in 1864. John Osborn operated a hotel for members of the government, and his sons John and Neri served as pages in the first territorial legislature. Running errands in the crude log Capitol building was an adventure for the boys; one of Neri's memories involved delivering a message to a Council member from his wife miles away in Granite Dells: "The Indians attacked us viciously this morning, but we drove them off. Send us some more powder."

Too much of this kind of excitement convinced the Osborns that the peaceful Salt River Valley might be a better place to settle. After years of harassment by the Tonto Apaches, they left their burnt-out farm, taking the Wickenburg road south to a totally different life.

John Osborn lost no time establishing a ranch in what is now downtown Phoenix and immersing himself in community affairs. He donated land for a school; it was at that school that his son Neri met his future wife. Marilla Murray was one of eight sisters newly arrived from Texas. Almost every year for the next decade a Murray sister married a local man, adding considerably to the family life in the frontier community.

In 1882, Marilla married Neri, and the home they created in the young town of Phoenix was almost the stereotype for the nineteenth century western family, an amalgam of gentility and opportunism. Marilla was not one to allow bad language or vulgarity in her house, but her husband was a rambunctious character who delighted in arguing politics with his siblings, his friends and even his children.

Sidney was the first of six children. They grew up in an atmosphere permeated with politics, especially the issue of statehood. They acquired an insider's knowledge of mining, cattle ranching and real-estate development; their father made his living from those fields when not involved in public service. Neri held a series of offices at both county and territorial levels.

Young Sidney attended the public school, delivered newspapers and played football, but his interest in politics began early. At twelve, he served as a "Captain of the Junior Warriors for (William Jennings) Bryan and Free Silver." The silver-tongued orator lost that election and many more, and the Arizona boy came to admire his tenacity. It was about this time that he wrote in the flyleaf of his history book: Sidney P. Osborn, Governor of Arizona.

At fifteen, Osborn followed the family tradition of serving as a page in the territorial legislature. In 1901, the surroundings were more luxurious than Neri's log cabin; the new Capitol was just completed, a state-of-the-art building complete with elevators, carpets and gas-and electric light fixtures. The sessions were shorter in the days before air-conditioning, leaving plenty of time to study at Phoenix Union High School.

After graduation Sidney landed a dream-job for a future politician: John Wilson, the territorial delegate, took him to Washington as his secretary.

**Young Sidney P. Osborn**
**Circa 1889**

**Sidney P. Osborn, Secretary of State**
**1911**

Washington was a big revelation to a provincial from the wilds of Arizona, and watching the antics of Congress amazed him as much as everything else in the Capitol. A territorial delegate was really only a glorified lobbyist, though his secretary probably assumed the same duties as congressional staffers today: ironing out problems, answering mail, and greeting local firemen. Trying to obtain statehood was the one issue Arizona's delegate addressed, and though Wilson was hard-working and well-meaning, he was rather dull beside the flamboyant Marcus Aurelius Smith, who won the office from him in 1904. This brought Sidney back to Phoenix, where he decided to try the newspaper business.

In the days when newspapers were unabashedly partisan, a journalistic background was an acceptable and effective way to enter politics. Osborn was still a political fledgling when the Maricopa County Democrats chose him to run for delegate to the Constitutional Convention of 1910. The Democrats swept that election, making him the youngest delegate in that wildly liberal and progressive body. He rubbed shoulders with future governors George W. P. Hunt and B. B. Moeur, helped draft the all-important recall article, and worked hard for women's suffrage.

In 1911, Arizona voters gave their approval to the new constitution, but another election was necessary to remove the recall article and ensure the President's signature. That second election also chose the first officials of the new state. Constitutional Convention President Hunt ran for Governor; Sidney was a candidate for Secretary of State. Despite a landslide of abusive editorials from the *Arizona Republican*, the Democrats again swept the boards, and Sidney Osborn moved into an office he would hold until 1918.

While the Secretary of State's duties were largely ceremonial and clerical, Osborn did a good job. He seemed to enjoy his work, and was especially happy to accept what the *Republican* called a "cute little petition" for the women's suffrage amendment, which became part of the Arizona Constitution in 1912. The next year, the first nominating petition signed exclusively by women voters endorsed Osborn to succeed himself as Secretary of State.

In 1912, Osborn married Australian-born Marjorie Falconar Grant, whom he met when he was a Capitol reporter and she was a stenographer in the governor's office.

He was re-elected in 1916, the year that George Hunt and Thomas Campbell slugged it out for the governor's chair. Osborn loyally visited Hunt in exile, though he did not share all Hunt's views. He kept a prudent but unheroic low profile during the Bisbee Deportation in July of 1917.

In 1918, George Hunt knew he could not win and did not run. His choice for Democratic candidate was Fred Colter. It was no surprise when Sidney Osborn also ran for governor; he had been mentioned as a candidate for the last two elections and the time seemed right, with the giant Hunt out of the field. But he lost to Colter in the primary, who in turn lost to Thomas Campbell in the general election. It was the first of a series of defeats that would brand Osborn for a perennial candidate.

The year 1919 found Sidney widowed—Marjorie had died in the flu epidemic of 1918—unemployed, and nearly broke. He tried a lot of things: real estate, mining, insurance, and a disastrous experience in the Valley's Great Cotton Boom, which left him with a debt that took years to pay off. He married, a second time, Gladys Smiley, whose rather short life was troubled by crippling arthritis.

Six years seemed about as long as he could go without running for governor, so in 1924, he tried again. Unfortunately, Hunt was once more incumbent and running, and Osborn was trounced a second time.

Once again he returned to the newspaper business. He became editor of *Dunbar's Weekly*, a paper that had championed him for over a decade. As editor of a feisty journal of political thought, Sid poked fun at pompous politicians, excoriated boondoggles, and pointed the finger at local scandals more sensitive papers avoided. In 1932, he supported Dr. B. B. Moeur for Governor. Moeur's success resulted in considerable advances for Sidney Osborn; he was appointed Chairman of the Democratic State Central Committee, and later received a federal appointment as Collector of Internal Revenue.

Perhaps it was the visits to Washington he made as an Arizona Somebody, instead of the secretary of an Arizona almost-Nobody, that started him thinking about the U.S. Senate. Henry Fountain Ashurst had held his seat since

**Inauguration of Sidney P. Osborn**
**1941**

**Governor Sidney P. Osborn**
**Credit: Arizona Department of Library**
**Archives and Public Records**

the dawn of statehood, and he seemed more at home in Foggy Bottom than in Coconino County. The year 1934 found Sidney Osborn challenging and losing to "Five-syllable-Henry," as Ashurst was known for his lavish vocabulary.

Osborn might have wanted the Senate, but he would have to wait six years to oppose Ashurst again. He would not run against Carl Hayden, whose term ended in 1938, because Hayden was a personal friend and political ally. Replacing him would not serve the state; working with him would.

The 1938 governor's race was an odd one: several "firsts" and one "last." It was the first election in Arizona in which one of the candidates barnstormed by plane. It was the first Arizona election in which a Hunt candidate did not finish. Tragically, this was because the Hunt candidate, his longtime friend and aide C. M. Zander, died in a crash in his pioneering airborne campaign. This happened a scant week before the Democratic primary, and the three remaining candidates, Secretary of State James Kerby, druggist Robert T. Jones and editor Sidney P. Osborn tried to maintain the dignity of mourning while pondering furiously over the future of the dead man's votes.

Osborn received an endorsement from the Zander forces, but observers remember how that success backfired: rumors circulated that the Osborn people had made a deal with the Zander people. The implication of political maneuvering before the body was cold counted against him. The primary, which was to have been a race between Osborn and Kerby, went to Jones.

To add excitement, Kerby declared the election was rigged and that he would run as an independent, but nothing much came of that. Jones won and Osborn lost, but for the last time.

His campaign workers remember that Osborn was almost serene in his acceptance of this loss and in his conviction that he would win ultimately. The late Evo DeConcini, who directed Osborn's Tucson campaign, recalled: He said, "Well, we'll wait, we'll run again, he's sort of like Lincoln. You know, Lincoln was defeated I think 15 or 16 times. He finally ended up as President of the United States. And maybe Osborn read that too, and said, 'Darned, I'm not going to fail, I'm going to make it."

The 1940 election was staid and quiet compared to the preceding one, with the exception of one rowdy meeting where Osborn opened his remarks: "When I began running for Governor a short time ago . . . ." This innocent comment opened a floodgate of jeers and jokes about his unending quest for the governor's chair. He finally reworded his statement: "During the time I have been running . . ." which resulted in general, and more sympathetic, laughter. But he won. And continued to win, with ever greater majorities, three more times.

Sidney Osborn had waited to be governor of Arizona his whole life, and he knew what he wanted to do. He had watched all his predecessors, admired some, criticized others, and probably spent more time Monday-morning quarterbacking than anyone in Arizona political life.

He had magnificent plans for Arizona, and in his first year he experienced the double jolt of having executive power and of facing the opposition of the State Legislature. The Fifteenth Legislature was totally composed of Democrats, and the Governor suggested the Democratic Platform of 1940 as their Legislative agenda. It wasn't that easy.

Osborn was a fervent new-dealer, an enthusiastic disciple of Franklin Roosevelt. Arizona was dragging itself out of the depression and the new governor meant to find jobs, to build roads, to upgrade social services and to make the government work overtime. The Legislature was far more conservative, peopled with incumbents whose Democratic policy was "pinto," and far more laissez-faire than the national ideal. Conflict was inevitable.

And there was the Colorado River. For twenty years, due to a lack of leadership and an excess of political infighting, Arizona had held back from joining the Santa Fe Compact. This agreement committed Colorado River basin states to cooperation in use and development of that river's resources. Osborn finally succeeded where six previous governors had failed, and convinced the State Legislature to work with the other compact states. This allowed Arizona to participate in federal development of the Colorado River Basin, and paved the way for the Central Arizona Project.

When he made an appointment to office, he demanded a signed and undated letter of resignation from the candidate. However,

**Governor Sidney P. Osborn with his Mother,
Marilla Murray Osborn**

**Gladys Osborn, Sidney Osborn
and Aide, Jack Hirsch, on a
Trip to San Francisco in Search of a
Cure for his Illness, 1947**

he almost never interfered with departments once he felt they were properly staffed.

As a former newsman himself, the governor understood and respected the press, but he had one gadfly problem: Bill Turnbow. He wrote the *Gazette's* political gossip column, "Under the Capitol Dome" (the name of the column had been originated years earlier by Osborn himself in the long-defunct *Phoenix Sun*) and it was considered unkind and untrue by many observers. When appeals to integrity and good sportsmanship failed, Osborn simply broke all his news stories to the press after three p.m., the *Gazette's* deadline.

David Brinegar, a Capitol reporter at the time, remembers that Osborn's door was always open, that he would wave reporters in to talk to them; the formal press conference was a contraption of the future. Osborn answered his own phone, greeted thousands of people by their first names, and was proud to be called "Sid" in return. It was an easier time, with a small-town atmosphere.

World War II postponed many projects Osborn had hoped to complete, and saddled him with war powers that brought their own problems. He tried to balance national and local defense and security needs with his own longtime respect for personal liberties. The Japanese Internment camps, which unloaded thousands of west-coast Japanese-Americans in the Arizona desert, presented a far more difficult challenge than "cleaning up" Phoenix so that troops stationed nearby could visit.

War's end found Arizona emerging a different state than it had been—more populous, more urban, more conservative. Demands for housing, jobs, highways and airports flooded the governor's office. Working closely with the Congressional delegation, especially his old friend Carl Hayden, Osborn helped design modern Arizona. His vision often brought him in conflict with the State Legislature, and when they balked at his plans, he vetoed legislation, called unprecedented numbers of special sessions, and used radio and personal appearances to bring his message to the electorate. His favorite—and most effective—tool was simple persuasion. He had warm friends of every political and economic stripe, and he could often convince them to do what he felt was best for the people of Arizona.

Those who rightly credit Sidney Osborn with bringing Arizona's water policy into the twentieth century sometimes forget that he was also in the forefront of human rights, care for the unfortunate, education, and labor relations. He literally risked his life in an attempt to negotiate a settlement during a potentially disastrous strike in 1947.

The greatest challenge of his life was the crippling disease which ended it. Ameotropic lateral sclerosis, sometimes called Lou Gehrig's disease, gradually destroyed his health, leaving him paralyzed and speechless. Only sight and hearing were left unimpaired, and a total consciousness of the hopeless situation. Osborn faced this last crisis with the same stubbornness that had characterized his earlier life. He refused to despair; he refused to resign. He worked every day, under the most trying circumstances, until his death on May 24, 1948. The words of Evo DeConcini expressed the feelings of many who knew him: "The best governor Arizona ever had . . . he went out of office in glory and sadness, a great loss to Arizona."

## SOURCES

*Arizona Republic*

*Arizona Republican*

Brinegar, David. "In the Line of Duty"

DeConcini, Evo A., "Hey!  It's Past 80!" *A Biography of a Busy Life*, Tucson, Arizona, 1981

*Dunbar's Weekly*

Finnerty, Margaret, "Sidney P. Osborn, 1884—1940: The Making of An Arizona Governor," Master's Thesis, Arizona State University, Tempe, Arizona

"Governor Sidney P. Osborn's Last Year." *Journal of Arizona History*, Autumn, 1975

Gunther, John, *Inside U.S.A.*, New York, Harper and Brothers, 1947

*New York Times*

*Phoenix Gazette*

Wagoner, Jay J., *Arizona Territory, 1863—1912:  a Political History*, University of Arizona Press, Tucson, Arizona, 1970.

Original research and documents collected are housed in the Arizona Room, Hayden Library, Arizona State University.  The collection includes copies of letters, news clippings, photos, ephemera and transcribed oral history interviews.

**Governor Daniel E. Garvey**
**Credit: Arizona Department of Library**
**Archives and Public Records**

# DANIEL E. GARVEY

## 1948—1951

*Author: Christine N. Marin*

When an interviewer asked Dan Garvey what he was most proud of in the years he spent in public service, he didn't hesitate to say that he was proud of his "reputation of being honest." It was this trait of honesty and sincerity that kept Garvey in public office in various capacities for over 40 years.

Daniel Edward Garvey, Democrat, became the state's eighth governor upon the death of Sidney P. Osborn, who died of ameotropic lateral sclerosis, or Lou Gehrig's disease, on May 24, 1948. Later that year, Governor Garvey won election to a full term as governor.

Dan Garvey was born in Vicksburg, Mississippi, on June 19, 1886. He attended St. Aloysius College, and upon graduation, he went to work for the Yazou and Mississippi Valley Railroad as a clerk. As a young man of 23, he moved to Tucson in December, 1909, where he found work as a railroad clerk for the old Epes Randolph Line. On February 20, 1912, Governor Garvey married Thirza Jeannette Vail, daughter of Zach Vail, a prominent and wealthy pioneer Tucson cattleman. The couple had three children, one of whom died of injuries caused in a automobile accident in 1937. In their early marriage, Garvey and his wife lived in Globe, where he worked for the Arizona Eastern Railroad, Globe Division line as an accountant. He later moved to Phoenix in 1924 to work as an accountant for the same railway. His office was located over a drug store and on the fourth floor of the old Goodrich Building on the corner of Central Avenue.

The railroad company transferred Garvey to Tucson, and later to Guadalajara, Mexico, for approximately three years. Another transfer brought him back to Tucson, where he worked as a clerk and auditor for the Southern Pacific Company for the next several years.

Garvey thought he "would work for the railroad company for the rest of [his] life," until he began his political career when he became a member of the Tucson City Council. In 1927, he was chief deputy assessor of Pima County. By 1929, he had become deputy county treasurer, then later served four years as chief deputy beginning in 1931. In 1934, Garvey was elected Pima County Treasurer and was re-elected to that post two years later, resigning in 1938 to become city treasurer of Tucson. The following year, he was appointed assistant secretary of state, holding that position until his appointment as Secretary of State by Governor Sidney Osborn to fill out the unexpired term of Harry M. Moore, who died unexpectedly following an appendectomy in April, 1944. Garvey announced his own candidacy for election to that same office and easily won the election. Under Garvey's direction, the Office of Secretary of State made for itself an enviable record of efficiency and economy and an outstanding reputation for courtesy in all of its contacts with individual citizens who had business there.

One of the most unusual titles Dan Garvey held at this time was "acting for the acting governor." It happened in 1939, when Governor Robert Jones travelled to New York to attend a national governors' conference. Harry Moore, as Secretary of State, was acting governor, but also left the state on a vacation trip to visit his brother in Missouri. Thus, Garvey, who was acting secretary of state, while Moore was acting governor, became the acting acting governor. Garvey became governor without being elected to any state office! Little did he know that this position would be his officially within a few years. Death removed Sidney P. Osborn from that office in 1948, and placed Dan Garvey as the

**Governor Garvey Looking over the Teletype News**
**Credit: The Phoenix Newspapers, Inc.**

new post-World War II Governor.

Garvey's first official act as acting governor upon Osborn's death was to issue a proclamation designating a state-wide 30-day mourning period for Sidney Osborn. He also pledged to the state's citizens that he would continue the politics and the principles advocated and adopted by Osborn, and also vowed not to disturb any of his political appointments.

But immediately upon the death of Osborn, legal questions developed as to the exact official status of Dan Garvey. Was he governor, or acting governor, *and* secretary of state? This was the first time in state's history that a governor had not served his full term, and there was a question over whether Garvey could legally become the new governor. Arizona's constitutional provisions regarding succession, never before tested, somewhat indefinitely and non-specifically stated merely that in the event of a governor's death, the duties of that office would devolve upon the secretary of state. Garvey was both: Secretary of State, and Governor, and was prohibited by law from surrendering either of them. The Arizona Supreme Court subsequently decided that Garvey was only acting governor. In November, 1948, however, Garvey was elected governor of the state of Arizona in his own right.

Garvey quickly assumed an easy approach to solving various state problems, especially those focusing on water legislation. He gained approval of the Central Arizona Water Project Authorization Bill by the Senate Interior Committee, and brought hope that the Colorado River water would one day irrigate Central Arizona farms. His goal was fulfilled when he initiated the historic signing of the Upper Colorado River Basin Compact, which allotted 50,000 acre-feet of water annually to the small portion of Arizona within the basin.

During his term, he also sought support for and gained congressional approval of the Central Arizona Project, which brought an additional 1,200,000 acre-feet of Colorado River water into Maricopa and Pima Counties, and at an estimated cost of $758,585,000. Not one to take complete credit for his water accomplishment, Garvey gave credit to Senator Carl Hayden, Congressman John R. Murdock, and U. S. House of Representative Harold A. Patten for bringing reality to the development of a system which would relieve Arizona's most drastic water shortage problem.

Turning his attention to other state matters, Governor Garvey proposed that jurisdiction of the Indian reservations pass from federal to state government, thus improving conditions for the Indians. Garvey felt that with Indian lands on the state tax rolls and free from federal control, development of natural resources could be advanced more rapidly. With those rich oil and ore resources on reservation land being untapped and underdeveloped and virtually unexplored, both the Indians and the state of Arizona could prosper from a change in status. Unfortunately, Garvey's ideas seemed too premature, and his attempts to make the Indians full citizens of the state were not always successful.

In other developments, Governor Garvey sought additional ways of gaining economic relief from tax bills for the state and initiated a program for counties to prosecute fathers who willfully deserted or failed to support their own children. Garvey felt that such cases cost the state approximately $90,000 per month, and felt such costs were too exorbitant. He even went so far as to propose that county road camps be established so that these men who deserted their families would be identified and put to work as forced laborers on various projects which would benefit the needs of each county.

Governor Garvey remained a tireless and industrious worker who pursued his executive duties with deliberateness and perseverance; yet, he always remained calm and ever mindful of his responsibilities to the people of the state that he so cherished. He never sought fame for himself, but worked for the benefit of others whenever he was called upon to do so. His administration saw the Children's Colony established, the expansion of higher education developed throughout the state, and also saw the revision and the modernization of the state's highway code.

Governor Garvey was unsuccessful in the primary race of 1949, but left his executive office with dignity and with great pride in his accomplishments. In 1950, he was named Arizona administrator of the federal Reconstruction Finance Corporation before his 1955 appointment as state examiner by Governor Ernest W. McFarland. He held that

**Governor Garvey—Fishing
Credit: Arizona Department of Library
Archives and Public Records**

latter post until his retirement in January, 1969. Governor Daniel Garvey died on February 6, 1974, having remained a loyal and dedicated public servant to his party, his constituents, and to the citizens of the state.

## SOURCES

*Arizona Politics: The Struggle To End One-party Rule,* Arizona State University, Tempe, Arizona, 1986

*Arizona Republic,* 1948-1950

Garvey, Daniel, Papers, Arizona Collection, Hayden Library, Arizona State University, Tempe, Arizona

Garvey, Governor Dan E., Oral History Transcript, Arizona Collection, Hayden Library, Arizona State University, Tempe, Arizona *Phoenix Gazette,* 1948-1950

Goff, John S., *American Biographical Encyclopedia,* Volume 5: Arizona, Phoenix Paul W. Pollock, 1981

Shadegg, Stephen C., *Arizona Biographical Dictionary,* Cave Creek, Arizona, Black Mountain Press, 1983

**Governor John Howard Pyle**
**Credit: Arizona Department of Library**
**Archives and Public Records**

# JOHN HOWARD PYLE

## 1951—1955

*Author: Dr. Robert Gryder*

Thomas Miller Pyle, the father of John Howard Pyle, was born December 22, 1878, in Macon County, Missouri, in a log cabin where he lived with his parents until he was six years of age. His family moved to Walnut, Missouri, then to Grundy County, and finally settled in Oklahoma.

Thomas attended the State Teachers' College at Edmonds, Oklahoma, from 1901-1903. During this time he met Mary Sue Anderson who had come from Kentucky to live with her brother and his family. Mary Sue's brother, William Anderson, was a minister of the Baptist Church in Wellston.

After finishing school at Edmonds, Thomas went to Wyoming where he worked for the C.B.&Q. Railroad doing steel construction for $2.50 a day. He also worked on cattle ranches. Arrangements were made for Mary Anderson to come to Wyoming where they were married December 3, 1904. In 1907, they moved south to Waco, Texas, where Tom worked with the Brazos Iron Works as a boiler maker and steeple jack while attending Baylor University in the College of Theology from 1908-1912. At this time he became an ordained Minister of the Baptist Church at Wellston, Oklahoma.

While Mary Anderson Pyle and Tom Pyle still lived in Sheridan, Wyoming, their first child, John Howard, was born on March 25, 1906. A second son, Thomas Virgil, was born on June 12, 1908, in Waco, Texas. In 1915, they moved to Chandler, Oklahoma, and it was here that their third son, Maurice Jerome, was born August 13, 1915. His father's influence on Howard was profound because one of Howard's outstanding characteristics was his high moral tone in all of the many activities of his life. In later years he was a caring and understanding lay leader and teacher in the Baptist Church.

## EARLY YEARS

At an early age, Howard earned his pocket money. At the age of 11, he was a church janitor with a $2 monthly salary. Later, he delivered newspapers for an additional $1. In later years he became a registered Republican and earned $18 a week as a mechanic. While singing in his father's church choir, he decided to invest money in his voice; this investment made it possible for him to become a radio singer in 1924. He was graduated from high school at Columbus, Nebraska. Later he appeared as a soloist.

When his family moved to Tempe, Arizona, in 1925, Howard realized that the necessities of earning a living required changing his dream of a future in music. While living in Tempe, Howard entered the Atwater Kent search for musical talent and advanced to the semi-finals in San Francisco. He became a traveling time-keeper for the Southern Pacific, a real estate salesman, secretary for the Tempe Chamber of Commerce, Tempe correspondent for the *Arizona Republic* and publisher of promotional literature for the community of Tempe. These early assignments as a young man proved helpful to him as he assumed future leadership roles on state, national and international levels.

In 1929, the *Arizona Republican* acquired Station KFAD, assumed its management and changed the call letters to KTAR. This move was an opportunity to combine a knowledge of music and show business with his growing experience in advertising, so the position of program director was asked for and obtained. On October 22, 1930, he joined the staff of Station KTAR. During the next twenty years, he advanced from staff announcer and writer to vice president and stockholder of one of the

**Howard Pyle, NBC War Correspondent**
**The End of World War II**

**(left to right) Mary Lou, Mrs. Lucile Pyle, Governor Pyle, Virgina—New York Harbor, July 16, 1954**

Southwest's largest and most successful broadcasting enterprises, the Arizona Broadcasting System. During these years, the voice of Howard Pyle became familiar to almost every Arizonan within earshot of a radio set. He was known especially for his "Arizona Highlights" and "Poetry Exchange," regularly scheduled programs over a period of many years.

On August 9, 1930, Howard Pyle was married to the former Lucile Hanna of Tempe. They have two daughters, Mary Lou and Virginia. Mrs. Pyle continues to make her home in Tempe. In 1935, Howard Pyle became co-founder of the annual Grand Canyon Easter Sunrise Service, long internationally famous, and continued as its producer for more than 20 years. Perhaps one of the high points of his work year came as the first morning rays of the sun appeared into the Grand Canyon on each Easter Sunday.

## WORLD WAR II

In 1945, with World War II drawing to a close, he widened his scope of interest to include international affairs. He was commissioned to present a series of broadcasts from the World Security Conference in San Francisco where, through daily contacts with the leaders of over 50 nations, he brought the people of Arizona first-hand knowledge of the developments which led to the formation of the United Nations. During this assignment, he was accredited to the Pacific as a war correspondent. He interviewed hundreds of Arizonans in the service, from Borneo to Tokyo, and sent these transcribed interviews home for broadcast. In addition, the National Broadcasting Company contracted with him for a series of special releases that made radio history. He reported the Ie Shima arrival of the Japanese surrender party for all four major United States networks; he was the first radio correspondent to arrive in Japan with our ground forces. He was with the 11th Airborne Division when it was landed at Atsugi near Yokohama. Following the signing of the surrender aboard the "Missouri," he personally was invited to cover General Jonathan Wainwright's return to the United States.

## THE POLITICAL ARENA

In 1950, Howard Pyle entered the political arena and, by 3,000 votes, became the second Republican governor in the history of Arizona as a state. He had never held political office before. He served two two-year terms, winning the second by 53,000 votes and losing the third by 13,000. He worked in the White House for four years where he served in the nation's nerve center before beginning a 15-year stint with the National Safety Council. "The National Safety Council was the most rewarding of all experiences," he said, listing the council's life-saving accomplishments during his stewardship.

Pyle spoke highly of his four years with the Eisenhower team. "He was such a tower of integrity, such a proven leader and such a decision maker that when he walked into the White House he didn't have to prove all that," Pyle said. Pyle's debut as governor, nevertheless, was cause for speculation by some political observers. "They thought I was a political accident," Pyle said. But Pyle said he, former Senator Barry Goldwater and former House Minority leader John Rhodes knew what they were doing when they set out to make Arizona a two-party state. For too long, they thought, Democrats had dominated the state.

"What's happened since my governorship gives me more pleasure than anything during my governorship," Pyle said. "There's 30 years of maturing; conservative political philosophy of the state. We did what we set out to do." After his second term as governor, Pyle accepted a position in Eisenhower's administration as head of state and federal relations. Then he was involved in studies of highway accidents, followed by responsibility for the president's security in 1958.

In 1959, Pyle accepted a position as president and chief executive officer of the National Safety Council, which instituted the internationally recognized defensive driving course, led the drive for car safety belts as standard equipment, and began campaigns against drunk driving. "By any comparison, this was the most rewarding of any of my public pursuits," Pyle said. Pyle retired at age 68 after 15 years with the council. That, he said, is when he got busy. "I'm 81 years old,

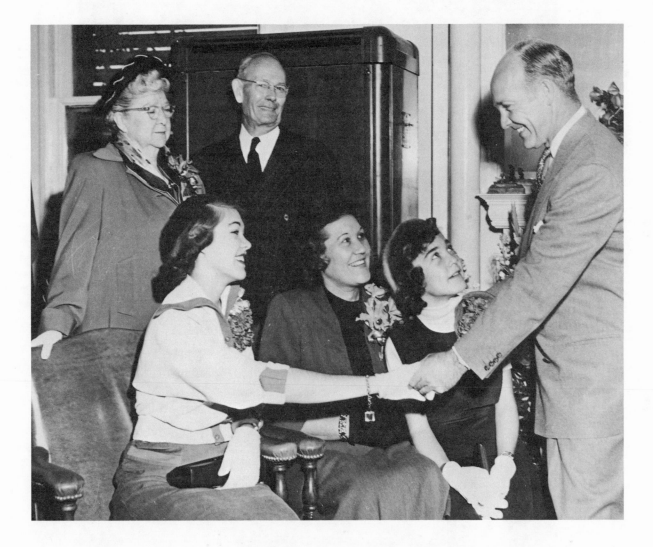

**Second Inauguration**
**(left to right) Rev. and Mrs. T. M. Pyle (parent's of**
**Howard Pyle), Mary Lou, Lucile Pyle, Virgina,**
**and Governor Howard Pyle**

**Seated left—Governor Howard Pyle, Standing—Congressman John J. Rhodes, Seated right—Senator Barry Goldwater**
**Credit: KTAR Broadcasting Company**

and I really enjoy life," he said. "To reach the age of 81, hail and hearty, to have a lovely family—really takes good fortune."

YEARS IN RETIREMENT

In 1974, addressing the 15th Annual Arizona Historical Convention on "The Hazards of Public Life" at the Hotel Westward Ho, Pyle said:
"If there is one thing certain about public life, it would be that you can never be certain about the way it's going to turn out. If you step into public life from the business world where you have been accustomed to some measure of efficiency, you are very promptly stuck with some large-size disappointments."
In reflecting on his four years as governor, Pyle said there is always opposition in the state's highest office and "you cannot enter into public life without expecting personal injury."
In 1977, Governor Pyle was tapped by Bob Finch Post, Veterans of Foreign Wars to receive the coveted "Citizen of the Year" title and plaque, post commander Eugene Beauperland announced. Beauperland remarked that Governor Pyle was the unanimous choice of the VFW selection committee for the Citizen of the Year honor, which has been given since 1950. Beauperland further remarked that "Mr. Pyle has devoted almost his full time at being the local 'good neighbor.'"
In a 1979 interview at his home with Richard Charnock, United Press International, Pyle remembers that, "I never planned to do anything I ever did. I never went to college a day in my life. I learned what I learned in the university of day-to-day experience." Howard Pyle held honorary degrees from Arizona State University at Tempe, Chapman College in Los Angeles, the University of Redlands at Redlands, Lebanon College, Lebanon, Pennsylvania, and Bradley University at Peoria, Illinois. "I tried never to take any opportunity lightly," he said. "I worked at each job as if it were the last thing I was going to do."
Charnock remarked that his visit with Howard Pyle began in a 10 by 12 foot den, its walls covered with pictures—many autographed—of everybody from General

Jonathan Wainwright to President Dwight D. Eisenhower. An adventure in itself, even a 30-minute guided tour through this room does not begin to show what he saw or the experience he has known. First as an administrative and then as a deputy assistant, he served in the White House from 1955 to 1959 and knew such history makers as John Foster Dulles. His photo album of the time shows pictures signed by Dulles and by then Vice President Richard M. Nixon. "He (Nixon) was undoubtedly one of the most—if not the most—politically experienced members of the administration, he recalls. But he acknowledged Nixon had a flaw that many believe contributed to his political demise: "His personality was against him under almost every circumstance."
As first speaker on Heard Museum Guild's Annual Lecture Series, Pyle's topic was "Reflections on an Arizona Governor —25 Years Later."
Short Creek in those days was a tiny settlement on the Arizona border, isolated from the rest of the state by the Grand Canyon and an inadequate highway system. It was inhabited by "renegade" members of the Mormon faith who were still practicing polygamy, despite the fact that both the church and the federal government had outlawed multiple-wives marriages. "Mohave County officials had appealed to the state for aid in accomplishing a quick crackdown, not only on the basis of the federal law but also because of inequities and violations of school taxes and management," he said.
"We put together a task force of 250 men, moved into Short Creek in the middle of the night, took away the wives and children and arrested the men, some of whom had five wives and 27 children. End of Short Creek; end of my governorship," he wryly explained. "It was neither the time nor the place to do what we did." Eventually, he said, all the men were released by a judge he himself had appointed because the state government had never implemented statutes to prosecute violations of Section B of the U.S. Constitution. The moral, he said, is "You get killed quicker in government doing your duty than turning your back." Those who could remember those days, could also remember "the sheer insanity of running for governor on the Republican ticket in this state that had been Democratic

**Governor Howard Pyle and President Dwight D. Eisenhower**

since its inception."

"A little known fact about my entrance into the political arena was that Barry Goldwater and I had agreed that government is a necessary thing and that we would do what we could to help the party on the outside become the party on the inside. In fact, we had even agreed that since Barry had a store to run here in Phoenix, he would run for governor and I would run for the U. S. Senate. However, in 1950 I was drafted during the Republican state convention as the party's candidate for governor. My wife, Lucile, who is a Democrat with whims of iron, told me she didn't mind my running—she was just afraid I would be elected.

"The GOP had a very modest organization, but Barry had an airplane. We campaigned all over this state, all day, every day. It was a big breakthrough when six people in Winslow showed up for a campaign breakfast, and no one took us very seriously. Furthermore, I was running against the late Anna Frohmiller, a Democrat who had earned the right to gubernatorial aspirations as few Arizonans ever have, during her service as state auditor. The last few days before the election I went into every barber shop, bar and beanery in town, shaking hands, kissing babies, the whole thing. I didn't know what Barry was doing then, but now I do. He was laying bets with his legions of Democratic friends. The GOP won that election by 3,000 votes, but NOBODY won like Barry did. Nonetheless, the Democratic state legislators still couldn't believe the GOP or I were threats.

"In 1952, Eisenhower ran for president, Barry ran for the U.S. Senate, John Rhodes ran for congressman and I ran for governor. We shellacked 'em.' I take no credit (for vitalizing the two-party system in this state); it had to start somewhere. It did and rolled on and on," he said. But his part of it ground to a halt in the 1954 gubernatorial election when Short Creek and the Democratic candidate, Ernest McFarland, defeated him.

"And Short Creek is still here," he quipped, "only now it's called Colorado City." The political battle of opposing forces peaked during Pyle's last term as governor, when he broke up a polygamous colony at Short Creek, which was south of the Utah state line.

"I lost the next election because I insisted on doing what I thought should be done, I never believed the Short Creek episode was the deciding factor in that election, but many people believe it was." He said serving as governor also taught him progress comes slowly, adding, "a lot of the problems we had during my governorship into the 50s are the same problems we have now."

The following statement appears to reflect Governor Pyle's thoughts on his first four years as Governor. "Power politics, prejudiced and selfish one-party rule guarantee only one thing for sure—government by favoritism and cronyism. This is the kind of government that caused a federal judge called to Phoenix in the surplus property cases to declare: It seems certain that of well over one million dollars of donated property (some think a great deal more) only a trickle reached the schools. Where did this property go? How did it slip through the state's control? Those who could answer will not. But they will try desperately to restore the sort of government by favoritism that let it happen. Arizona cannot afford preferential government again. Working together we got rid of it four years ago. Let's keep right on having government for all the people. I'm ready." Howard Pyle.

FINAL THOUGHT

Governor Pyle was a unique individual serving as Governor of Arizona during the 1950s. His deep love and devotion to his family, his state and his nation have insured his high place in the history of this state. His death occurred in a Tempe hospital, November 29, 1987.

SOURCES

*Arizona Biographical Encyclopedia, Volume* III, Paul W. Pollock Publishers, Phoenix, Arizona, 1981, p. 269
*Arizona's Men of Achievement, Volume I,* Paul W. Pollock Publishers, Phoenix, Arizona, 1958, p. 294
Charnock, Richard, *He's Rubbed Elbows with Famous, Traveled in U. S. Highest Circles, Tempe Daily News,* October 2, 1979
Charnock, Richard, "Ex-Governor Pyle, 73, is Retired in Name Only," *Mesa Tribune,* September 30, 1979
Dakes, Judith, "Pyle Looks Back on Full,

Busy Life as Arizonan," *Phoenix Gazette*, May 8, 1987

"Ex-Governor is Citizen of the Year," *Tempe Daily News,* April 25, 1977

Goff, John S., *Arizona Biographical Dictionary,* Black Mountain Press, Cave Creek, Arizona, 1983, p. 83

Grezesiek, Lori, "50-Year Affair with Politics Not over for Ex-Governor," *Phoenix Gazette,* August 20, 1980

*History of Arizona*, Volume III, Lewis Historical Publishing Company, Inc., New York, 1958

Law, Glen, "Hazards of Public Life, Ex-Governor Recalls Career," *Phoenix Gazette,* May 5, 1974

Pyle, Howard, "The Man for the Job!" Undated

Pyle, Thomas Miller, *The Pyle Family,* dictated to Evelyn R. Pyle, 1967, pp. 1-3

**Governor Ernest W. McFarland**
**Credit: Arizona Department of Library**
**Archives and Public Records**

# ERNEST W. MCFARLAND

## 1955—1959

*Author: Karen K. Kroman*

Ernest W. McFarland was born October 9, 1894—near Earlsboro, Oklahoma. His parents were modest prairie farmers who had settled on the Pottawattomie Strip soon after it opened. Their family home was a mere one-room cabin on the Pottawattomie Strip. His parents had always longed for education and were determined their four children would have the opportunity to learn.

Ernest enjoyed school but while in grade school and high school, farm work often caused him to miss school. This often troubled Ernest, but he made no complaints and respected his parents. He understood the welfare of the entire family must come before his own.

Ernest went to school in Earlsboro, Oklahoma, until the 11th grade. He then had to go to school in nearby Seminole. He went with a cousin, Elbert Swan, who would ride on horseback with him to school. The boys got jobs doing janitorial work at school to help earn expense money, but, unfortunately, they were fired after Ernest caused the furnace to blow up one night. This was the only job Ernest McFarland was ever fired from!

Ernest McFarland was a friendly boy who developed great friendships with many people who became prominent persons in the country. Ernest McFarland graduated from Earlsboro High School in 1914. He graduated third in his class. Incidentally, his graduating class totalled only three students.

In the spring when Ernest was graduating from high school, his father tried to earn additional money by putting in a larger cotton crop. Ernest's father gave Ernest and his cousin an interest in the crop so they could earn money for college, but, as so often happens, an Oklahoma drought hit and the boys did not make any money.

Determined to go to school anyway, Ernest attended East Central Normal School in Ada, Oklahoma. Times were tough and Ernest had practically no money so he began to do odd jobs with friends Earl and Henry Weston, Frank Thompson, and William Ingle who had similar situations. His financial situation remained so desperate that when he became friends with the school administrator, Charles Bryles, Bryles loaned Ernest $25 to complete the term.

McFarland managed to earn a two-year certificate to teach school and landed a teaching position in a town called Schoolton, Oklahoma, in the northern part of Seminole County. The town had only a post office, drugstore, general store and a one-room school. The Schoolton School had a reputation for tough kids who it was reported ran off the previous two teachers. Ernest was still just a kid himself. Apprehensive, but anxious, Ernest decided to be a strict disciplinarian. Shortly after arriving, he overheard some of the older boys say that the teacher seemed pretty tough and could probably "whip the tar out of them." After that, Ernest knew he would become a success.

His favorite subject was mathematics, which he majored in at both East Central and Oklahoma University. His mentor, Charles Bryles, suggested to Ernest that there was no nobler profession than teaching. For a time he decided he would teach. He was kept busy teaching mathematics at Ada High School while he was a student at East Central. He considered engineering as a career, but he could not pass the mechanical drawings which would have been required. At the end of his first year at the University of Oklahoma, he chose law as his profession. Additional jobs Ernest had while attending college were: teacher, janitor, grocery deliveryman, law librarian, and insurance salesperson.

Ernest McFarland was awarded a

**Governor McFarland at the Ground-Breaking Ceremony
for the Addition to the State Capitol
July 31, 1957
Credit: Arizona Department of Library
Archives and Public Records**

Bachelor's degree in the Spring of 1917 from Oklahoma University. Soon after Ernest graduated from college, World War I broke out and he joined the Navy. He was in the Navy until after Armistice. Ernest returned to Oklahoma but soon decided to move to Arizona.

Ernest traveled to Arizona by train with $10 in his pocket. He stopped in El Paso, Texas, to send a telegram stating his arrival time in Arizona. He found out the telegram would cost $1.10 and decided he could not afford it. He left the message he intended to send with the girl in the telegraph office and to Ernest's amazement, the girl sent it anyway. She evidently felt sorry for him and paid for it herself. The train stopped in Bowie, Arizona, where he decided to buy a sandwich. The price of the sandwich was 70 cents—too much for him with only $10. He got back on the train without the sandwich.

Young McFarland ended up in Phoenix on May 10, 1919, with the original $10 he had when he left Oklahoma. Fortunately, after interviewing with an employment agency in Phoenix, he secured a job as a teller with Valley National Bank a few days after arriving. He worked for the bank for several months and then decided to return to school to study law at Stanford University. Before leaving for Stanford, he filed a homestead claim for 160 acres of land north of Casa Grande.

While at Stanford in 1919, he met a girl named Clare Collins. She was talented in music and according to Mac "could have made the grand opera." Unfortunately, she developed a throat condition which lessened her singing ability. Clare graduated from Arizona Teacher's College in Flagstaff and intended to return to music. Clare's family homesteaded near Florence where she taught school. Ernest and Clare were married in 1925. They had a happy but unfortunate life together. They lost two children shortly after they were born. Clare became ill and depressed after the loss of her children and died in 1930.

After his last semester at Stanford, he was employed by the law office Phillips, Cox, and Phillips. As a law clerk he worked for Judge John C. Phillips who later became Governor of Arizona. After law school and passing the Bar, a young Ernest McFarland started practicing law in Casa Grande. The economy was bad at the time which did not help in developing his law practice. During that time, the big concern for the area was the need for more water for irrigation and cheaper, more efficient pumps. The farmers of the area were working for the San Carlos Dam which later became the Calvin Coolidge Dam. This was the beginning of an interest in water and water rights which would carry through the rest of Ernest McFarland's life.

With little or no work in law, Ernest played in politics with the election of 1922, hoping to get a better job after the election. He became acquainted with politics and met some of the best people he had ever met. In January, 1923, Ernest was appointed Assistant Attorney General under John W. Murphy with whom he worked for two years. He argued his first case in front of the Arizona Supreme Court.

In 1924, Ernest ran for Pinal County Attorney. At that time the law required the County Attorney and other county officials to reside in the county seat. Ernest won the election and moved to Florence. McFarland's legal residence remained in Florence.

While in the Office of Attorney General, McFarland learned a great deal about many things including prohibition and bootleggers. Mac became tired of pushing people into jail so he decided to run for Judge of the Superior Court in Pinal County. In 1930, he ran against Judge E. L. Green. Mac lost the election by only 80 votes.

During his term as Attorney General, McFarland appointed Tom Fulbright as his deputy. Mac and Tom Fulbright became friends and at the end of Mac's final term as Attorney General (he served three terms), Tom and Ernest became partners in a law firm in Florence. The office was named McFarland and Fulbright.

They had a good practice but Mac felt it important to advance his career, and politics was the best way. In 1934, he ran again for Superior Court Judge. McFarland had been successful in law but losing the 1930 election by only 80 votes made him want to try again. He had acquired more capital which would help him in his campaign. In 1934, he was nominated in the primary and ran in the general election without opposition. In January, 1935, he became Superior Court Justice.

While Justice of the Superior Court, Mac tried many important cases, two of which were water rights cases involving the entire state of Arizona. These cases lasted approximately three months each. In addition, he was the attorney for the San Carlos Irrigation and Drainage District. His knowledge about water rights and its importance for Arizona was ever increasing.

During this time, Ernest met and married another teacher named Edna Eveland Smith. Edna taught mathematics and history at Florence High School. The couple had a daughter named Jewell.

Ernest McFarland's philosophy of life was always, "If you want to get ahead in life, you either need to be smarter than the average person or willing to work harder than the average person." He said that he had often seen those who believed they were smarter than the average person fail, so he always tried to work harder.

McFarland served for six years on the bench. He then ran for U. S. Senator against Henry Ashurst. Senator Ashurst had held his office for 28 years and was tough opposition. McFarland, however, launched a surprise campaign against Ashurst counting on the fact that the cities of Phoenix and Tucson would rather vote for a man who did not live in the opposing city and used a total of $12,000 for his campaign. He had made a host of friends while serving as the Assistant Attorney General, County Attorney, and Judge of the Superior Court in Pinal County. He called upon his friends' support which helped him in his campaign.

He traveled extensively state-wide renewing old acquaintances but waited until the last minute to tell his friends of his plans to run for Senate. He always felt timing was important and always used it to his best advantage. Both men retained their integrity and ran a clean race. McFarland beat Ashurst by almost 2 to 1 but the relationship remained a friendly one.

After Mac went to Washington, Henry Ashurst and Mac became good friends. Mac once said to Henry, "Well, Henry, it's a good thing I didn't know you so well at the time of the campaign. That would have made it difficult for me to run against you."

McFarland's first committee assignments in the United States Senate were: Indian Affairs, Interstate Commerce, Irrigation and Reclamation, Judiciary, and Pensions.

Soon after Mac arrived in the Senate, a resolution was introduced by Senator Gerald R. Nye which called for an investigation of the motion picture and radio industries relative to propaganda. A committee was appointed to hold hearings on the matter. Senator Wheeler believed Mac would not cause trouble. Mac had been placed on the committee because Senator Wheeler had placed all abolitionists on the cases and Mac was considered a silent member "who would keep his mouth shut."

Mac proved to be a blessing for the film industry. He spoke out against the committee and said that those who had made the accusations against the films in question had not even seen the films. Mac then asked in the hearing if the investigation was for publicity. This first major assignment gave Senator McFarland national publicity. Many people considered McFarland as somewhat of a hero.

Mac was also asked to serve on the Subcommittee on Communications. By 1937, Western Union and Postal Telegraph systems controlled the field. They had made huge investments in equipment which was necessary to maintain with an annual payroll of $85,000,000. However, rapid advancements in the telephone, radio, teletype, and airmail were quickly making the Western Union and Postal Telegraph systems obsolete. By 1938, the Postal's net losses amounted to $4,042,518 and were climbing. Postal had begun to borrow money from the Reconstruction Finance Corporation. The RFC soon realized that the Postal would never be able to repay and proposed a merger. Hearings were conducted and many began to realize how serious the situation had become. Dealing with the FCC gave Mac his initial interest in communications. He later organized the Arizona Television Company and made application for and was granted a license for Channel 3 which went on the air March 1, 1955.

The G. I. Bill of Rights was, in Mac's eyes, one of the most important events in his career as a Senator. Mac had seen many soldiers out of work after World War I and while World War II was going on, he felt it necessary to see that this sort of misfortune for those who had served the country not happen again. Mac's argument was that during war time many men and women leave their civilian lives and families, jobs, and educations to fight for our country. Therefore, Mac sponsored

**Governor Ernest W. McFarland during a Press Conference
at the State Capitol with his Secretary Mrs. Mabel Stallcup
March 28, 1958
Credit: Arizona Department of Library
Archives and Public Records**

and introduced legislation to financially assist our returning veterans.

McFarland was chosen Senate Majority Leader through a simple set of circumstances. In 1950, attendance for Senate sessions by Democrats was particularly low because of their busy work with committees. Senator Langer appointed a committee of 12 to watch the floor and make certain that a Democrat was on the floor at all times in case a vote came to the floor. The Democrats appointed Mac to make sure that someone was in the Senate at all times. Mac was the one everyone was counting on. Eventually, it became easier for Mac to be there himself than to keep other Senators on the floor.

The Congress adjourned September 23, 1950, and the two most likely candidates for majority leader were not re-elected to the Senate during the November elections. The Democrats were appreciative of the hard work Mac had put forth, so he was encouraged to run for Majority Leader in January, 1951.

While Majority Leader, Mac developed his own committee comprised of standing committee chairmen whom he invited to lunch with him once a month. He also invited all freshman Senators to his monthly lunch meetings. He believed that a good deal of business could be handled during these informal sessions. Mac always felt it important to say as few words as necessary during the sessions of the Senate. He did not believe in wasting time with unnecessary speeches. During Mac's reign as Majority Leader, much work and even more bills were passed. One bill which did not pass, much to Mac's dismay, was one requiring equal rights.

Prior to Roosevelt's death, Mac sat next to Harry Truman for two years in the Senate and became quite good friends with the Vice President. This friendship benefited Mac through much of his work in the Senate. Mac was Senate Majority Leader during President Truman's administration.

Mac felt his official role as Senate Majority Leader required two different duties—his responsibilities as Majority Leader and also to represent his state. He also deemed it appropriate to convey his views of the Senate to the President. This was not always easy because many chose to report only the good news to the President. Mac believed this was a disservice.

"I never hesitated to present views contrary to those of the President in our conferences. As I've said before, I think that too frequently, the President is only told things people think he wants to hear. I would like to emphasize that it is not pleasant to present a view contrary to that of the President in such conferences."

Water rights were again to be an issue for the Senator from Arizona. Coming from Oklahoma and witnessing some of the worst droughts ever recorded in the history of our nation, McFarland recognized the need for water for Arizona's farmers, industry, and the people who live there. While in the Senate, he requested an assignment on the Irrigation and Reclamation Committee. Mac appeared before the Appropriations Committee asking that money be appropriated toward an investigation of the most feasible route to bring Colorado River water to central Arizona. He became an expert on water laws and was often employed as a special consultant for various state agencies. His adversaries admitted his undeniable knowledge on water rights.

Communications was another important interest for McFarland. After McFarland's final term in the U. S. Senate, he accepted an offer of the communications companies to help solve the problems of the industry. Because of Mac's extensive work in the Senate on communications, this was an important experience for the former senator.

In the Winter of 1954, Mac's friends urged him to run for Governor of Arizona. Arizona had been a Democratic state and had only twice elected Republicans to the office. The second Republican was Howard Pyle, who currently held the office. Pyle had been elected in the landslide election which elected so many Republicans. Mac knew that the people who knew him would vote in his favor but the large number of newcomers to Arizona (and there were many) were Republican.

McFarland believed his popularity within the state would defeat Pyle outside of Maricopa County. He knew that he could still win the election if he lost by only 5,000 votes in Maricopa County. Mac's strategy included conducting a poll in the county to see how badly Pyle would beat him. The polls were conducted twice; one poll stating Pyle would beat him by three to one and the other by four to one. Mac quickly decided the polls were wrong and ran anyway.

One of the issues for the campaign was Governor Pyle's efforts to change some of the state's offices to be appointed rather than elected. Mac believed that the people could choose their officials. An *Arizona Republic* and *Phoenix Gazette* poll just prior to the election indicated that Pyle would win the election by 15,000 votes. Mac won the election by 12,238 votes.

During McFarland's campaign for Governor, he stressed opportunity for all to have jobs, homes, and a few enjoyments. He believed that Arizona should win the right for additional Colorado River water. During his inaugural address to the legislature on January 10, 1955, he called attention to the fact that the state's population had grown 35 percent in recent years but the volume of business had increased by only a small percentage.

Mac soon began to stress the economy in solving some of Arizona's problems. He requested the Board of Regents make every effort to trim their requests for the 1956-57 budget. Mac also requested the state allowance for ADA be increased. This issue caused differences among the House and the Senate. He was pleased when a compromise was reached. Also, there were recommendations for future building of the state's colleges and universities. These buildings, in Mac's assessment, were built in time to save the state the good deal of money because of rising costs. In total there were 139 bills passed during the first session of the legislature. Among topics which were discussed by the legislature was eliminating the law which gave the state a preferred claim or lien against assets of deceased welfare recipients.

While McFarland enjoyed the job of ribbon cutting for various functions, he tried to delegate this job wherever possible. He soon learned that all of his time could be easily consumed by giving in to every request which was made of him. He did, however, enjoy being around the people and made it a point to visit different parts of the state to hear about the issues which were prevalent in their area. He held a series of informal open houses throughout the state during the Summer of 1955.

McFarland was concerned about Arizona's tremendous highway fatality record. During the holiday season of 1955 he called for the National Guard's assistance in helping to keep fatalities to a minimum. They were put on duty patrolling the state's highways with successful results. It was estimated that 19 lives were saved during the holiday season of 1955 compared with 1954.

During McFarland's administration, businesses began to call attention to the fact that in most other states they had eliminated state sales tax on sales made to the Federal Government on products produced in their particular state. Sperry-Rand had stated that they could not compete with other businesses within the industry while this tax existed in Arizona. They went as far as to threaten to move their business out of the state and gave the State of Arizona until December 15, 1955, to make a decision. Governor McFarland was compelled to eliminate the tax but knew that the state relied on the revenue generated from the tax. Before it could be eliminated, it had to be determined where the additional revenue for such a large tax cut would come. The legislature was deadlocked on December 9, 1955. Mac thought that a compromise was in order. First, he recommended a limit be set on the types of industry which would be excluded from the state tax. The industries which would not be required to pay were manufacturers, modifiers, assemblers, and repairers. He also recommended passage of a user tax which would be a sales tax on purchases from outside Arizona. The legislature passed the bill.

Other bills signed into law under McFarland's first term in office were assurance of racial opportunities, appropriations of $350,000 for the Arizona Interstate Stream Commission to finance a study for the most feasible way to bring water from the Colorado River to central Arizona, and assistance in preventing juvenile delinquency.

Another McFarland project was the study of a possible seaport for the State of Arizona. It was felt and believed, by the board who was studying the project, that Arizona was too close to the sea without having access to it. Mac believed Arizona's access to the Gulf of Mexico would benefit both Mexico and Arizona. This project would have, of course, required the cooperation from Mexico. Agreement was never reached. This project was considered by some to be of great significance and would open the entire Southwest's future.

During 1956, a decision to locate the Glen Canyon Dam was reached. With a great deal of planning and negotiation, Arizona won the right to locate the dam at its present location just south of the Utah border in Arizona. The Glen Canyon Dam routed and continues to route commerce through the state. Without this decision, the town of Page, Arizona, would not exist.

According to Ernest McFarland, the 1956 governor's campaign was his easiest. He ran against Horace Griffen and received the highest vote for any state or national candidate in Arizona history.

Governor McFarland began his second term by recommending the development of a State Parks and Recreation Board to protect the natural landscapes and wildlife in Arizona. He also recommended the building of new state capitol facilities and a new stadium for Arizona State University.

At the end of the 23rd Legislature five major bills became law. These were: (1) an addition of 25 staff members to the Highway Patrol; (2) an appropriation to continue the fight against California for a fair share of Colorado River water; (3) establishment of a State Parks Department; (4) funding for a new stadium at Arizona State University; (5) continuation of the study of the state's tax laws.

McFarland's concern for the mining industry of the state caused him to appoint Sam Morris as Chairman of the Arizona Copper Tariff Board. Because the price of copper has a good deal to do with the economy of the state, the Arizona Copper Tariff Board was appointed to prepare legislation which would reinstate a four-cent copper tariff, which was originally adopted in 1932, for periods of time when the copper price dropped below thirty-two cents. Because the copper price was down during this particular time, it meant that the taxes which were normally carried by the mining industry were no longer being collected. After the lengthy fight for the copper tariff, the Western Governors' Conference unanimously approved a resolution supporting the tariff.

Governor McFarland strongly supported user taxes for cigarettes, alcohol, and fuel. He believed that the revenues from these luxury items could be generated to help in education and also in highway improvement and would not affect the average family. When Governor McFarland took office, the state and county employees had a six-day work week. Governor McFarland recommended giving state and county employees a five-day work week, which was later passed by the legislature.

Governor McFarland called attention to a problem within the State Senate. The Senate's system of committees was operated by the committee chairmen. If the chairman did not see fit to introduce the measure to the committee, the measure would never be discussed by the committee and, therefore, never by the Senate as a whole. Governor McFarland was not in the position to solve the problem. However, he did bring attention to the problem which was eventually resolved.

When it came time for Governor McFarland to either make the decision to run for re-election or declare he would not run, he decided not to run. He was a firm believer that a governor should hold a limited number of terms and believed that a governor's "building an organization" was not good for the state. He instead chose to run again for the seat in the Senate occupied by Senator Barry Goldwater.

McFarland did not agree with many of the tactics used by Senator Goldwater and Goldwater's campaign workers. Ernest McFarland lost the Senate election after a race which tested McFarland's commitment to "never defame the character of one individual in order to further my own gain." He proudly retained his dignity and self-respect.

Ernest McFarland believed all three branches of government to be equal and soon after his defeat for the seat in the Senate, he announced his intention to run for the Arizona Supreme Court (at that time Supreme Court Judges were elected). A position on the Supreme Court was one of his life-long dreams and one to which he was proud to be elected.

During his service to the Arizona Supreme Court, which began in 1964, his typical day began at 8:00 a.m. and finished at 6:30 p.m.. He felt fortunate to serve with other judges whom he considered as "good friends." He believed, "the court had a duty to look at the long run effects of its decision."

Among the many controversial cases which were heard by the Arizona Supreme Court during McFarland's era were: *State v. Miranda* in which the issue was the rights of

the accused. This case was eventually overturned in the United States Supreme Court. In *Phoenix v. Civic Auditorium*, the city of Phoenix was considering the building of an auditorium which the city would lease back from private individuals. This arrangement would circumvent the constitutional limitation on city debt. In *Sanders v. Folsom* McFarland questioned the state's tax rates which did not make certain funding available for local schools.

Ernest McFarland retired from the Supreme Court in 1971, and was honored by a dinner. The May, 1977, edition of The *Stanford Lawyer* stated in its introduction, "This issue is dedicated to Ernest W. McFarland, Stanford University School of Law, Class of 1922." The issue also contained the statement, "The Editors of the *Stanford Law Review* take pleasure in dedicating this issue to a truly uncommon man and alumnus— Ernest W. McFarland." This was the first time an issue had been dedicated to any individual.

Ernest McFarland is the only person in the history of Arizona who has served in all three branches of government. In 1974, Ernest McFarland purchased the old Pinal County Court House which had been built in 1878 and served not only as a courthouse and jail but also as a county hospital. The old adobe structure had been condemned and was due for demolition. The McFarlands then transferred the deed to the Arizona State Parks Board and a trust fund was established by the McFarlands to fund its reconstruction.

Ernest W. McFarland died in Phoenix, June 8, 1984.

In 1954, a radio commentary program on KOY by Jack Williams, a Republican who was later to become governor, said this about Ernest McFarland: ". . . from the days when Governor McFarland wound up the 'fair haired senator' for the committee investigating the moving picture industry until today; he has moved in the forefront of great endeavor, and although Senator Barry Goldwater tripped him, he in turn tripped Governor Howard Pyle! And that was no cinch victory. Governor McFarland ran the shrewdest, smartest political race that I have ever seen in this state.

"All of which leads me to say tonight, that I think when the history of Arizona is written, Governor McFarland may loom larger on its political horizon than any other name.

He may not be smart, but he's governor. He may not be smart, but he has been U. S. Senator, and a lot of the smart ones can't say either. Plus the fact that he's liable to get the Colorado River for us through his last suggestion of having the state go ahead and build it. That was a 10 strike, a suggestion . . . coming with all the force of the governor's office behind it. Even the Republicans who have been selling state's rights and to get away from big government can't complain on this one. He has stolen their thunder. It's not a new and brilliant suggestion, but like so many of Mac's actions, it was released at the ideal time and under the ideal circumstances. If he isn't smart, I'd like to be whatever he is—even if you just call him lucky."

## SOURCES

*Arizona Biographical Encyclopedia, Volume III*, Paul W. Pollock Publishers, Phoenix, Arizona

*Arizona's Men of Achievement, Volume I*, Paul W. Pollock Publishers, Phoenix, Arizona, 1958, p. 270

"Ex-Governor Gives State First Courthouse in Pinal," *Arizona Republic*, December 31, 1974

Goff, John S., *Arizona Biographical Dictionary*, Black Mountain Press, Cave Creek, Arizona, 1983, p. 66

*History of Arizona, Volume III*, Lewis Historical Publishing Company, Inc., New York, 1958.

McFarland, Ernest W., *Mac, The Autobiography of Ernest W. McFarland*, 1979.

**Governor Paul J. Fannin**
**Credit: Arizona Department of Library**
**Archives and Public Records**

# PAUL JONES FANNIN

## 1957—1965

*Author: Dr. David H. Lynch*

Paul Jones Fannin was born in Ashland, Kentucky, on January 29, 1907. He was brought to the state of Arizona when he was only eight months old due to his father's health. He grew up on West Moreland Street in Phoenix and attended Phoenix Union High School. While in Phoenix Union, he was a member of a student body that included such business, social, and political figures as Bob and Barry Goldwater, Orme and Bob Lewis, Mel Goodson, Robert Creighton, Jack Williams, Newton and Harry Rosenzweig and Royal Marks.

Fannin was graduated from Phoenix Union High School in 1928, then attended the University of Arizona for two years. He then went on to Stanford where, as an economic major, he was graduated with a Bachelor of Arts in business administration in 1930.

Immediately after graduation, he returned to Phoenix to enter his family's hardware business. Later he joined his brother Ernest to establish the Fannin Gas and Supply Company, which marketed petroleum and agricultural chemicals throughout Arizona, New Mexico, Idaho and the Republic of Mexico. During the initial years of the business, Fannin and his brother worked extremely hard and experienced some privation. For example, they often had to sacrifice their own needs to meet their payrolls. Even during this difficult time, they were able to pay bills and maintain a high level of customer service. During this especially difficult period of time, Fannin revealed himself as an honest and sincere individual.

Although Fannin served as an executive officer of the company for 20 years, he also dedicated himself to many community organizations, an activity he has continued throughout the years. He has actively participated in such organizations and activities

as Chamber of Commerce, Thunderbirds, industrial development projects, Community Chest, YMCA, The Arizona Business and Education Partnership (ABIEC), and Red Cross.

He married Elma Addington on May 6, 1934. Elma, a native Phoenician, has had to assume the several roles of wife, mother, and campaigner. Their family consists of a daughter, Linda, and three sons, Thomas N. Fannin, Paul R. Fannin, and William J. Fannin. They also have ten grandchildren and five great grandchildren.

## WORK AS A GOVERNOR

A conservative Republican, Fannin was not deeply involved in politics until he decided to enter the race for governor of Arizona in 1957, a decision that was influenced by the sale of his company to Suburban Gas Company and California Spray Chemical Company. During this time, he had clearly reached a turning point in his life. Aided by his friend, Barry Goldwater, he was elected in 1958 by 30,000 votes. He ran again for governor of the state in 1960 and in 1962 and won both times. He served as governor until January, 1965.

Fannin thought that his initial attempt at public office as governor would result in failure since at the time, registration favored the Democrats about eight to one. Fannin decided to run for governor because he wanted to participate in the building of Arizona recognizing as he did the state's economic and social potential. His victory in his first election was helped considerably by his operation of a successful business: his name was known in almost every community in the state. He also was active in sports as he had been a pitcher of a championship softball team sponsored by Funk Jewelers, which had played in dozens of

**Governor Paul J. Fannin**
**Credit: Arizona Department of Library**
**Archives and Public Records**

**Senator Paul J. Fannin goes to Washington, D. C.**

towns and cities and in national tournaments. His company sponsored the first live television sportscast in Arizona. The Fannin Sports Carnival sometimes ran as much as three hours a day broadcasting football, basketball, fast pitch softball and other sporting events. The first weather show in Arizona was sponsored by Fannin in the Fall of 1960 and Winter of 1961.

As governor, he had an open-door policy holding "open house" every business afternoon to hear from as many as 40 constituents a day without an appointment. Too, he was self-effacing, willing to give credit to those who could and would get the job done. He often chose the best men to aid him regardless of political affiliation, a trait which caused some friction between him and some fellow Republicans. He felt a deep obligation to maintain the opportunities for others that had enabled him to succeed in his own business. His political philosophy as governor was simple: to successfully accomplish a basic purpose designed to benefit all of the people who were being served.

During his experience as governor, he learned to compromise. In fact, he had to since during his first term the Senate had only one Republican among its 28 members. It was not until his second term that the Senate started to cooperate with him since they were quite skeptical of Fannin when he first became governor.

During his three-term tenure, he faced many challenges. He worked tirelessly to attract industry to the state. He fought for better schools in Arizona by supporting a 50 percent increase in the state sales tax which raised $53 million that was put into the school system. He advocated the passage of legislation providing for a statewide tax equalization program. He led the fight for the establishment of a junior college system that would serve thousands of students across the state. His support of a junior college system got him into political trouble with many of the voters in Tucson as they saw a need for a medical school as more urgent than the creation of a community college system. Although he never opposed the idea of a medical school but only its urgency, several newspapers shocked him with such headlines as "Fannin Fights Medical School."

Perhaps Fannin's biggest problem during his tenure as governor—one that he himself discussed in some detail—was the limited power that he had. Actually, his authority was much less than his responsibility, for about 120 boards and commissions were operating in state government outside his power. Although he had the power to appoint members, after such appointment, he could do little to formulate policy or implement it. Consequently, his supervision of executive and ministerial offices depended far more on his persuasive power and the willingness of those people to be supervised than upon a procedural authority. In addition, he had little control over the budget, yet another difficulty he had to deal with.

Fannin believed that the greatest single event during his term as governor was the U.S. Supreme Court decision to allocate the Colorado River between Arizona and California, a decision which led to the creation of the Central Arizona Project (CAP).

While governor, he established the Arizona-Sonora West Coast Trade Commission, served as chairman of the Western Governors' Conference, functioned as a three-term member of the executive committee of the National Governors' Conference, and was a member of the President's Civil Defense Advisory Council, 1963 to 1964. He was a leader in the establishment of the Arizona Business Education Council.

## ELECTED TO THE SENATE

When Fannin's long-time friend and strong supporter Barry Goldwater decided to run for the office of President against then President Johnson, Fannin decided to run for ex-Senator Goldwater's office. Although Goldwater lost the election in 1964, Fannin was only one of two newly elected Republicans to the U.S. Senate. He was re-elected on November 3, 1970, for the term ending on January 3, 1977. Considered a workhorse, Fannin decided not to seek a third term as Senator when at the age of 68 he said that his health would no longer permit him to continue to work 12-hour days.

While in the Senate, he served as the ranking member of the Interior and Insular Affairs Committee, now known as the Energy and Natural Resources Committee, the Senate Finance Committee, the Senate Post Office and

(left to right) Senator Fannin, Governor Ronald Reagan
and Governor John R. "Jack" Williams

**(left to right) U. S. Senators Barry Goldwater, Carl Hayden and Paul Fannin**

Civil Service Committee, Labor and Public Welfare Committee, and was Chairman of the Republican Calendar Committee. A liaison with the White House on energy, he believed that energy was the most important problem facing the nation.

He did much work on the Foreign Trade Committee. He was especially concerned about the fact that the United States was spending billions on defense, which benefitted Japan, but Japan was flooding the American market with their goods while keeping goods from the U.S. out of their markets with high tariffs.

One of Fannin's significant accomplishments while in the Senate was his leadership during his first year in 1965 in killing a floor effort to repeal Section 14B of the Taft-Hartley Act, a section which permits states to enact right-to-work laws. Before the actual vote whether to repeal Section 14B, Fannin would run back and forth to communicate with Senators Russell and Dirksen. This activity helped him develop rapport with them and other senators which lasted through his years in office.

Of most importance to the people of the state of Arizona was his significant role as leader of the floor fight in the passage of the Central Arizona Project with his Democratic colleague, Carl Hayden, who appointed him floor manager of the bill for Arizona.

## RETIREMENT FROM ACTIVE POLITICS

After leaving public office, Fannin continues to be active in state and community affairs. He has been working hard for the development of different energy sources such as coal, geothermal, wind and solar and encouraged inventors who have developed devices for conserving energy in these fields. He served on the Central Arizona Water Conservation Board for six years retiring from that service December 31, 1988. He received the distinguished Arizona Heritage Award presented to him by the Central Arizona Chapter of the American Red Cross.

## SOURCES

*Arizona the Grand Canyon State: A History of Arizona Volume II,* Western States Historical Publishers, Inc., Westminster, Colorado, 1975, p. 832

Bartak, Bonnie, "Paul Fannin: Self-effacing but Effective," *Phoenix Magazine,* 1983, pp. 69+

*Catalog of Legal Aid Horrors,* Published by Fannin in Congressional Record, January 26, 1974

*Arizona Republic,* Congressional Directory of the 91st Congress, March 1969.

Falk, Odie, *Arizona, A Short History,* University of Oklahoma Press, 1970, p. 211

Farrington, Jr., Charles, "Paul Fannin, Governor of Arizona," *Arizona Highways,* 1959, pp. 3—5

"Paul Fannin is a Man Well Met Who Wears Well," *Tucson Daily Citizen,* September 9, 1958

Fannin, Paul J., Personal Interviews with John Myers, June 17, 23, 1989

*The Arizona Business and Education Conference Annual Report,* 1985

The Fannin Papers, University Archives, Arizona State University, Tempe, Arizona

The Office of Governor of Arizona Public Affairs Series No. 7, Bureau of Government Research, Arizona State University, Tempe, Arizona, 1964, pp. 5—10

Wynn, Bernie, "One Man's Opinion," *Arizona Republic,* October 23, 1970, p. 20

Wynn, Bernie, "Fannin Says Econology Classes Vital to U. S.," *Arizona Republic,* October 28, 1970

Wynn, Bernie, "Fannin Will Seek 3rd Term in Senate," *Arizona Republic,* April 6, 1975

Wynn, Bernie, "Fannin Decides Against Seeking Re-election," *Arizona Republic,* December 23, 1975

Wynn, Bernie, "Paul Fannin: Former Politician Still Works Actively for Arizona," *Arizona Republic,* November 26, 1978

(left to right) President John F. Kennedy, Senator Carl Hayden, Tom Chauncey, Representative Morris "Mo" K. Udall, and Senator Paul Fannin—Celebrating Senator Hayden's 80th Birthday
November, 1961

**Governor Samuel P. Goddard**
**Credit: Arizona Department of Library**
**Archives and Public Records**

# SAMUEL P. GODDARD

## 1965—1967

*Author: Dr. Donald J. Tate*

Biographical summaries refer to the twelfth individual to become Governor of Arizona as Samuel Pearson Goddard, Jr., Samuel P. Goddard, Jr., and Samuel P. Goddard. For many years he has been popularly known to Arizonans as Sam Goddard. His exposure to Arizonans during his nearly twenty years of residency prior to assuming office in 1965 revealed a person whose genuineness invited the name Sam Goddard.

The following description of him before taking office aptly describes Sam Goddard: His physical character and personality were stated as "a six foot three inch lean lawyer with a 'down east' reticence and a bit of skepticism in his cool penetrating brown eye." Additional traits were humor in his twinkling eyes and radiating friendliness but not hiding "the powerful driving force smouldering under his easy controlled manner."

The description of Sam Goddard continued. ". . . ask any of his acquaintances, friends, co-workers, employees—even his adversaries about him and you get a unanimous answer—greater personal integrity, a firm belief in himself and an insatiable desire to do for all those about him and to serve to the best of his ability, his state and his country."

Looking for a source of personality traits might take one to a person's ancestral locale, New England being the home of great grandfather John Goddard. He was a wagonmaster involved in hauling supplies to the front during the siege of Boston. Samuel Pearson, great grandfather on his mother's side, was a clipper ship captain. The family migrated west after the Civil War; his father was an officer during World War I. Attributing traits based on geography to Sam Goddard, born in Clayton, Missouri, in 1919, could be an amusing speculative exercise.

Following his pre-college years in St. Louis, Sam Goddard enrolled in Harvard, graduating with a B. A. degree in 1941. His future bride, born in Springfield, Illinois, enrolled at Wellesley. In due time, the courtship was underway. On July 1, 1944, he married Julia Hatch. They had three sons.

Soon after graduating from Harvard, Sam Goddard enlisted as a private in the U. S. Army Air Corp. In 1942, he attended Officer Candidate School in Miami, Florida, where he was commissioned. He left the service as a Major in 1946, but soon thereafter he was active in the Air Force Reserve from which he retired as a Colonel.

During World War II he served as an operations and communications officer in all theaters of operations; his military stations give him the opportunity to see parts of Canada, England, India and North Africa.

It was in the service when Sam made an early Arizona connection having met Senator Barry Goldwater at a new air base in Wilmington, Delaware. Years later old service friends prevailed on Sam Goddard to make a campaign donation to Barry Goldwater in 1958.

The second Arizona connection occurred when, "In the Summer of 1945, Mrs. Goddard came to Arizona to sit it out while her husband filled his next assignment in the South Pacific . . . ." Her husband was able to join her during a short leave, to celebrate their first Christmas in the Southwest. As they sat by the Christmas tree decorated with coins from Sam's world-wide collection for want of better ornaments, they looked around and decided Tucson was it. Sam Goddard returned to Tucson in 1946.

From 1946 on, Sam Goddard's many faceted life reached from home and family to varied community organizations, to state and

**Governor Samuel P. Goddard delivering a speech
Credit: Arizona Department of Library
Archives and Public Records**

national committees. He found time for personal interests such as music and art. Sam Goddard emerged from his myriad of experiences and associations with a cross-section of interested citizens to become the leader of the Democratic Party in Arizona.

Indications of the range of his talents and abilities marked his college career at Harvard. While a student there, he sang in the Glee Club and served on the Varsity Crew. His rowing prowess brought him the honor of being elected to the Rowing Hall of Fame in 1976—seemingly a long time after rowing at Harvard but not unlike delay recognition in other sports.

Earning an L.L.B. degree from the University of Arizona in 1949 and beginning the practice of law in Tucson opened the doors to opportunities for demonstrating his desire and drive in civic, people-caring, and political activities. Even as a law student, his leadership traits were evident—he was elected president of the Student Bar Association, University of Arizona, in 1949.

A chronology of his activities and memberships in organizations in both Tucson and Phoenix as well as regionally and nationally, clearly highlight Sam Goddard as a caring civic worker and leader:

1951—President and Charter member of the Tucson Festival Society
1958-59—Co-Chairman, Tucson Civic and Convention Study Committee Chairman, Tucson Civic and Convention Center Study Committee
1959—Chairman, Subcommittee in Fort Grant, Citizens Committee in Correctional Services Member White House Conference Committee, Children and Youth
1960-62—President, Tucson United Community Campaign
1961-63—President, Western Conference of United Funds and Councils
1963-69—Board Member, United Community Funds and Councils of America
1963-64—Board of Directors, Arizona Academy
1970—Coordinating Committee, Tucson Hospital Campaign Chairman, Tucson United Community Campaign
1967-68—Member of the Council, Regional Export Expansion Council

1970-80—Chairman, Independent Task Force, National Council on Philanthropy
1971—Chairman, Task Force on "Marking the System Work for America," United Way of America
1973-75—Chairman, National Academy for Volunteerism, United Way of America
1974-75—Chairman, Blue Ribbon Committee in USO, United Way of America
1980-86—Board Member, Independent Sector, National Council on Philanthropy

The activities listed in the above chronology extend beyond Sam Goddard's residency in Tucson, overlap his Chairmanship in the Democratic Party in Arizona, and extend beyond his Governorship of Arizona. Not listed in the preceding list are three items not closely related to those listed:

1968—Board Member, Associated Harvard Alumni
1968-71—Chairman, Nominating Committee, Harvard University Governing Board
1971-74—Vice President, Associated Harvard Alumni

Memberships in the following organizations reflect ongoing professional interests, long outstanding loyalties to individuals and to groups: American, Arizona, Pima County and Maricopa Associations; Phi Alpha Delta Fraternity; Reserve Officers Association; Air Force Association; American Legion; Veterans of Foreign Wars; National City Club; Old Pueblo Club; Harvard Varsity Club; and the National Rowing Foundation, of which he has served as Trustee. To these is added a specified religious advocation.

These memberships point to Sam's being a social being, as all successful political figures seem to be.

The identification of groups in which Sam over many years has been a worker and a leader show that he is committed to the welfare of individuals to continue maintaining loyalties, and to the advancement of certain institutions in total, he is a community man. The boundaries of his communities are: cities, regions, state, and nation and extensive activity in groups which lend to the success of geographical communities.

Sam Goddard is more than a man of

**Governor Goddard**
**Credit: The Phoenix Newspapers, Inc.**

communities—he is also a man of the professional world, the business world, and the political world.

In the professional world Sam Goddard has been a partner in two law firms, the first being Goddard, Gin, Hanshaw & Gianas, in Tucson, and the second being Goddard and Goddard, in Phoenix and Tucson. An observer of his office in Phoenix probably would conclude that Sam Goddard likes an office that reflects stability, that displays a pictorial history of prominent national governmental figures, that takes one back to days of beautiful hardwood floors and woodwork, as well as back to the days of elegantly solid furnishings. Certainly, one could speculate that these reminders of bygone days are a setting in which Sam Goddard ponders the present and projects the future.

Earlier biographical summaries, preceding his being elected as Governor of Arizona, mention his business affiliations.

One business venture that he particularly liked and for which he expresses enthusiasm was a communication business. In describing it Sam Goddard's eyes brightened, his smile deepened and he leaned closer from the other side of a conference table. The organizers of this business had roots and contacts to radio communications systems known to servicemen. He and his partner organized the first state-wide land mobile radio system with antennas scattered on many mountains. The company also operated in other states.

An interesting sidelight to this business was handling the necessary repair work. Servicing the antennas by driving and hiking to them took too much time. The solution was his becoming a licensed pilot to cover the locations in Arizona and other states and to Mexico, where the firm was also interested in communications.

Being a pilot also enabled Sam and Mrs. Goddard to visit more frequently in Mexico. The traveling in Mexico motivated Sam Goddard to learn their language, a language he continues to study by playing tapes in his automobile as he travels to and from his office.

Sam Goddard is also known as a proven man of the Democratic Party. He has been a precinct committeeman; and twice the Chairman of the Arizona State Committee, first from 1960—1962, second from 1978 to the present. He was elected Delegate, National Democratic Convention 1964, 1972, 1976, 1980, 1984 and 1988. He served as Democratic National Committeeman 1972—1978, and was a member of the Charter Commission Drafting Committee of the Democratic National Committee from 1972—75.

His reputation as a staunch grass-roots party man grew into working for the party on the national level.

On the state level he led the party through a metamorphosis from a "good ole boy" party to a party of the people, from a party that raised large amounts of money almost all of which came from lobbyists to a party that gets its money in small amounts from thousands of people, many of whom contribute more than once. They respond to telephone calls and to written communications. He developed a special category of contributors called "Power by the Hour"; this group is asked to give the party one hour's wage. He was responsible for another money raising program known as "Dollars for Democrats." This program emphasized the necessity for support from many individuals rather than from a few seeking special favors. He has led the way to a computer information systems to provide a better voter registration figures precinct by precinct. His efforts also resulted in direct mailing by the national Democratic party to party members in Arizona.

Sam Goddard's record of work in and for the Democrats from at least the time he was a law student shows that he is a dedicated believer in his Party and in good government. He is an analyst of influences and developments that have affected elections in general and the Democratic party in particular; he also sees emerging influences and developments. In short, he is a thinker. He has said, "We have to know where we come from and how we arrived here, or we won't be able to meet the coming challenges."

In his 1965 State of the State message to the Arizona Legislature, Governor Goddard clearly relates that he is a man of the state of Arizona. Embodied in this presentation are expressions of his humanity, vision, compassion, sense of current and future problems and values.

**Governor Samuel P. Goddard**
**Displaying Arizona's Unique Bird, the Roadrunner**
**Credit: The Phoenix Newspapers, Inc.**

Selected ideas from this address are:

The annual addition of thousands of new families cannot help but create unparalleled needs for new homes, hospitals, schools (classrooms) and additional sources of all kinds.

Our major investment must be in people.

We cannot afford to allow the State plant to run down through crowded schools, dangerous and poorly constructed roads and highways, superficial teaching, inattention to public health.

Urgency of assuring adequate water supply for the state's people, manufacturing, mining, agriculture.

The importance of the great natural heritage of such recreational facilities, fish, wildlife, grasslands, soil, forests, and water power—all inter-related with the water supply. Interests—economics, social, political of the less populated areas of Arizona as well as the populated areas.

Makeshift tax policies.

Make absolutely certain that no one class of taxpayers is required to support an unfair share of common expenses.

Assistance to the poverty stricken and improvement of their conditions of life.

Fighting discriminations of minority groups.

Importance of bringing capital into Arizona.

Recruitment of industry and faster industrial development.

Appreciation of the unspoiled beauty in Arizona. Importance of far-sighted, intelligent, and dedicated development of the majestic natural lands in Arizona.

Interest in the growth and development of Sonora in particular and Mexico in general.

Legislation providing medical assistance to senior citizens.

Honest work and a fair wage.

Enlistment of citizens who have demonstrated leadership abilities to assist state government.

Increasing complexity of problems in Arizona. The need for responsible, committed, and exuberant leadership.

Cooperation between the Legislative and Executive branches of government.

When Sam Goddard finished his term of office in 1967, he gave more time to his private life. Even so, the chronology of his activities show that even in 1967 he became a member of Regional Export Expansion Council—an activity that extended his horizons. Sam Goddard's life was one of extended horizons!

And since 1978, he has dedicated much of his time to leading the Democratic Party in Arizona, serving as the Party's chairman since that time, always looking to the future as he remembers his past.

## SOURCES

*Arizona Frontiers*, October, 1961, p. 13-14

Goddard, Samuel P., Governor, "State of the State Message," Arizona Legislature, 1965

Goddard, Samuel P., Interview with Dr. John L. Myers and Dr. Donald J. Tate, May 8, 1989

Winston, Rosanna, *Arizona Highways*, February, 1965 pp. 3, 4

**Governor John R. "Jack" Williams**
**Credit: Arizona Department of Library**
**Archives and Public Records**

# JOHN R. "JACK" WILLIAMS

## 1967—1975

*Author: Dr. Nelda C. Garcia*

"It's a beautiful day in Arizona. Leave us all enjoy it." With these words, one of Arizona's most listened-to voices, for more than forty years, would begin his daily radio commentary. The thirteenth governor, John R. "Jack" Williams, was a well-known personality, radio director, commentator, and column writer for the *Phoenix Gazette*. This three-term Republican governor of Arizona (1967 to 1975) was the first governor chosen by the people for a four-year term. A dedicated political conservative, he is a firm believer in the power of hard work and individual initiative to achieve personal goals.

Williams has been called a "master communicator," who made his daily "This and That" program well known on radio. He was not only a radio announcer for many years, but has also been a writer and public speaker. He has authored several publications: *From the Ground Up*, a collection of stories about Arizona mining; and *The Best of Jack Williams*, a booklet containing 50 of his best broadcasts. When Williams stepped down from public office, a colleague, Harry Rosenzweig said that now Williams "can look forward to his first love, which is writing."

Known primarily as a hard-lined political conservative, Williams has an impressive unpublicized record of aid to minorities, educational progress, health, welfare and other social programs. When he left office, he left a complete report on his administration, a 53-page, single-spaced typescript titled "Facts about Governor Williams and his Administration." Such a complete report on an administration had not been left by former governors of Arizona. And "If they had, the report on Williams would not suffer by comparison," stated an editorial in the *Arizona Republic*, January 1975.

## WILLIAMS—YEARS OF PREPARATION

Jack Williams identified with the poor and disadvantaged. He was born poor on October 29, 1909, in Los Angeles. While growing up in Phoenix, in the early 1920s, he developed an eye malignancy which was treated by Madame Curie. Although he lived in Mexico for several years, he was very familiar with Arizona and the city of Phoenix. He is an avid student of Arizona, its color, romance, and history as poignantly demonstrated in his stories of Arizona's mines and early mineral discoveries. When he moved to Phoenix with his family, he attended Phoenix Union High School and Phoenix Junior College. Then he began to work in Phoenix, joining the staff of Radio Station KOY in 1929.

## WILLIAMS—PHOENIX PERSONALITY

Williams later became station owner of KOY, and his participation in the affairs of the growing city of Phoenix increased. Williams was vice president of the Phoenix Housing Authority in 1944-47, president of the Phoenix Junior Chamber of Commerce in 1946, and a member of the Phoenix City Council. He was elected mayor of Phoenix in 1956 and served two terms. While mayor, he contributed to the updating of "The History of the City of Phoenix."

## WILLIAMS—PRIVATE AND PUBLIC PERSON

When Williams turned over the reins of the Governorship to Raul Castro in 1975, Williams and his wife Vera travelled to South America for an extended vacation. Political columnists and colleagues termed his trip "well earned" after several years of doing his part in

**"The Bolo Tie Proclamation"**
**(left to right) Jim Mayne, Duke Cameron, Bill Close**
**and Governor Williams**
**Credit: Arizona Department of Library**
**Archives and Public Records**

the private sector as a business executive, radio commentator, station owner, newspaper columnist, and lay leader for the Episcopal church. He has been described as "unselfishly involved in community service." He was named Man of the Year by the Phoenix Advertising Club in 1953 for his community service—an honor previously bestowed on Barry Goldwater, Howard Pyle, and Stephen C. Shadegg. Williams also did "his part" in the public sector by serving as president of the board of the Phoenix Elementary School District, Phoenix City Councilman, Mayor of Phoenix and Governor of Arizona.

While speaking to the Phoenix Rotary Club two weeks before his retirement, Governor Williams said that he realized he had been criticized for not being more emphatic in his leadership, but he stated his belief that only he was willing to allow his record to be judged by the perspective of history.

## WILLIAMS—POLITICAL PERSPECTIVE

Williams, who ran on the Republican ticket for governor in 1966, 1968, and 1970, was the victorious winner and served as the state's chief executive for seven years. He was a candidate with more name identification and greater political strength in Maricopa County, due to his years as the Mayor of Phoenix.

Largely as a result of his urgings in the 1966 campaign, Arizona, for the first time in history, elected a majority of Republicans to both houses of the state legislature.

As governor, it is said that Governor Williams maintained a low profile. The *Arizona Republic* commented that this was:

". . .partly because the state constitution doesn't give a governor very much power. But it's more because Williams is neither charismatic nor flamboyant. He is basically a team player who believes in appointing good men to top posts and then allowing them to run their departments."

While low-key, and perhaps lacking a flamboyant personality, Williams nevertheless accomplished many of his goals for the State of Arizona. Williams devoted his effort to achieving orderly economic growth. By emphasizing economic growth for the State of Arizona, during his three terms, Arizona enjoyed major results: employment rose from 548,000 to a labor force of 803,400 workers;

bank deposits increased two and a half times; and manufacturing employment increased by 103 percent.

Though known as a hard-line conservative, he tried to help laborers, farm workers, and minority citizens by balancing the budget, holding down taxes, and creating a favorable climate for industry, business, and commerce. As governor, Williams visited all 17 Indian tribes in the state, sat with their councils, talked with the leaders, helped them establish a plan for themselves in a "frequently hostile environment." He formed the Indian Development District of Arizona (IDDA), through which $50 million was spent on furthering economic development on Indian reservations.

Unlike many politicians, Williams did not choose to run for a fourth term. He never lost an election. He announced, during his third term, that he would retire at the end of that term of office. "I have served longer consecutively than other governors in Arizona's history, and during some extremely trying times."

## WILLIAMS—PROBLEMS

In the late Spring of 1973, a recall committee submitted 176,152 signatures to the Secretary of State for validation. During an ensuing investigation of the recall petitions, many of the signatures were found to be invalid, questionable, or gathered by circulators who were not registered to vote. The Attorney General ruled that no recall election should be held.

The recall issue revolved around a legislative act designed to provide unionization of farm workers under certain conditions. Williams' supporters claimed that the recall would not have changed the legislative act, and, the recall was aimed at the "wrong target," Williams. The catalyst for the act was a failed strike in Yuma, Arizona—when violence erupted in the cantaloupe fields as Teamsters and the United Farm Workers, led by Ceasar Chavez, clashed. Some continuous, sporadic violence occurred even after the recall was history. Stephen C. Shadegg, friend and colleague of Williams, wrote that this had been a "very difficult period for the governor emotionally, physically and financially. For seven years he had devoted all his energies and

(left to right) Paul Fannin, Roberto de la Madrid, Sam Goddard,
Ernest McFarland, Alejandro Carrillo-Marcor, Howard Pyle, Jack Williams
Credit: Arizona Department of Library
Archives and Public Records

135

talents to improving conditions for all the citizens of Arizona." Though the recall was defeated, this had been a very "trying time."

## WILLIAMS—PERSPECTIVE

When Williams announced that he would not run for a fourth term, many politicians expressed their opinion that Williams had done a good job as governor. *The Arizona Republic* stated that Williams could retire from the governorship with the knowledge of a "job well done," for he had served the state well. How well he had succeeded was evident from the fact that Governor-elect Castro requested many important incumbents from the Williams administration to remain in their posts. Raul Castro alluded to the "trying time" when he said that Williams, throughout most of his years in office, "had to face serious problems and many adversities."

Accolades were paid to Williams by other political leaders. "Jack has done a fine job," said former Phoenix Mayor, Milton Graham. "I believe Jack Williams has been a good governor," stated Russell Williams, for "he has served the state well and whoever fills his shoes will have a tremendous job before him." County Attorney Bob Corbin believed that Williams had done "a good job" with still a lot of things needing to be done. Jack Ross, another Democratic candidate for governor, called Williams "a dedicated public servant," adding that he thought that Williams had earned the right to retire and spend some time with his family. Ross especially noted that Jack Williams would now be able to do what he truly enjoys—writing.

In perspective, Williams was a governor whose life exemplifies a pattern of poverty to prominence, which as in all success stories, inevitably includes problems along the way. Politically astute, Williams nevertheless resolved the problems with grace and insight.

The communication talent of Jack Williams served him well before, during, and after his time as governor.

## SOURCES

Daws, A. George, *What Made Arizona—It's Men,* Daws Publishing Company, Phoenix, Arizona, 1920, p. 71

Meek, Walter W., *Arizona Republic*, October 10, 1970

*Notable of the West, Vol. 2,* New York International News Service, 1915, p. 606

Pollock, Paul W., *Profiles of Prominent Personalities,* Paul W. Pollock Published, 1977, p. 273

*Portrait and Biographical Record of Arizona*, Chapman Publishing Company, Chicago, Illinois, 1901, p. 1034

*Who's Who in Arizona*, Edited by Richard R. Reidy, Success Publishers, Scottsdale, Arizona, 1984-85, p. 279

Wynn, Bernie, "One Man's Opinion," *Arizona Republic*, October 16, 1970

Wynn, Bernie. "One Man's Opinion," *Arizona Republic*, November 6, 1970

**Governor Raul H. Castro**
**Credit: Arizona Department of Library**
**Archives and Public Records**

# RAUL H. CASTRO

## 1975—1977

*Author: Dr. Nelda C. Garcia*

The fourteenth state governor of Arizona, Raul Hector Castro, portrays the rise from humble beginnings to high honors. His characteristics, traits, and attributes comprise the portrait of a self-made man, offering proof of the American dream. In Latin America, where he served his country for thirteen and one-half years, he is known as the "Yankee Castro"—to differentiate him from "that other Castro." In Arizona, he is the only Hispanic governor to date.

## CASTRO, THE ACHIEVER

Raul H. Castro was born on June 12, 1916, at Cananea, Mexico, a small copper mining town fifty miles below the Arizona border, where he lived until 1926 when he moved to Arizona.

His family, forced to flee Mexico because of the 1916 Revolution, moved to and settled in Pirtleville, a border community in the Douglas area. Two years later during the Depression when Castro was 12, his father, a miner, died. Remembering this difficult period Castro recalled, "We really had to scratch for food." With his 12 brothers, 1 sister and his mother, a midwife, Castro spent the first 10 years of his life in an impoverished environment.

Trying "a little of everything" to make a living included working in the smelter with his brothers and panning for gold. Yet, he graduated with honors from Douglas High School, where he was an editor of the school newspaper and a star athlete. He also worked his way through college in Flagstaff plucking chickens and waiting on tables. He did find time for boxing and remained undefeated in intercollegiate boxing during his four years in college, winning the Arizona college middleweight crown in 1939. That same year,

at age 23, he graduated from Arizona State College and became a naturalized citizen.

## CASTRO, THE YOUNG PROFESSIONAL

Castro's early professional career was launched with U. S. citizenship, but was met with discrimination. Certified to teach, but not prepared to be told that "the school board passed a resolution not to hire any more teachers of Mexican descent," the young graduate faced the inevitable question of "What to do?" First, he left Arizona—riding freight trains, picking fruit, and staging boxing matches. Second, he returned to Arizona and joined the U. S. Foreign Service—taking charge of immigration and accounting in Agua Prieta, Sonora, where, again, he encountered discrimination when he was told, "A Mexican born with a Spanish name does not have much chance to advance."

Discouraged from a diplomatic career and disillusioned, Castro was still undaunted; he left his job and entered law school. To work his way through college, he started his teaching career by teaching Spanish, earning his doctor of jurisprudence degree from the College of Law at the University of Arizona in 1949.

Admitted to the Arizona Bar that same year, he practiced law for two years in Tucson where he became deputy Pima County attorney, from 1951 to 1954. He was elected Pima county attorney in 1954, re-elected in 1956, and served in that capacity for three years—when, in 1958, he was elected to the Pima County Superior Court.

The years of knowledge and experience, gained from criminal prosecution and from serving on the bench as juvenile court and superior court judge, rekindled a teaching commitment. During this time, he developed

**Governor Raul Castro on Horseback**

**Governor Castro and President Jimmy Carter**

an interest in counseling juvenile delinquents who appeared in his court, and a reputation for his firm but fair treatment of youngsters in trouble with the law. His "key-to-success" message for troubled youth was, "This country offers more opportunity than any other if you are willing to go out and sacrifice and work."

## CASTRO, THE AMBASSADOR/ DIPLOMAT/STATESMAN

Eighteen years after his first foreign service clerkship, President Lyndon Baines Johnson appointed him U. S. Ambassador to the Central American Republic of El Salvador. His performance was so outstanding that he was presented with El Salvador's highest award—the Matias Delgado Decoration.

Four years later, in 1968, he was given a second ambassadorship by President Johnson. He became U. S. Ambassador to Bolivia, in 1968, ending his diplomatic service in 1969 when President Johnson left office. Raul Castro re-assumed diplomatic service nine years later, on October 20, 1977, when President Carter appointed him Ambassador to Argentina.

In Bolivia, while a target for terrorists as his house was bombed twice, he nevertheless endeared himself to the Bolivians who christened him the "Ambassador on horseback." Astride a horse's saddle, he conducted countryside visits reaching out and shaking hands with the Bolivian citizenry, *peones*, and farmers.

After his 13.5 years of foreign service in El Salvador and Bolivia, Raul Castro returned to Tucson where international law practice was a natural pursuit for him. International cases sent him back to Central America, El Salvador and Guatemala, as well as to Arizona's southern neighbor, Mexico. Representing an American-owned railroad, whose assets were nationalized by Guatemala because of missing a payment on a $4 million mortgage, he tried to balance the scales on the assets taken from his American clients.

## CASTRO, THE CHALLENGER

A year after his second ambassadorship, Castro was the 1970 Democratic nominee for governor of Arizona. Castro's first governor's race against Jack

Williams was one of Arizona's closest; Williams received 50.9% of the vote, compared to Castro's 49.1%.

In the 1970 campaign, five major issues concerned Castro:

*Rising unemployment
*Air pollution
*Planned government organization and
    spending
*Leadership
*Human needs

Castro's 1970 vision for Arizona, if elected governor, focused on: 1) a state-wide kindergarten system, as provided in Arizona's constitution, 2) bilingual elementary education, 3) new water sources, 4) problem-solving meetings with mayors, 5) job creation and industrial growth, and 6) Arizona-Latin American trade.

Castro believed that leadership was needed for Arizona to combat its environmental, pollution, and drug-abuse problems. As Arizona governor, he planned to continue being what he always had been—a public servant—one sensitive enough to understand the problems of Arizona and energetic enough to do something about them.

Speaking in English and Spanish—to the delight of a bilingual audience in Douglas—Castro stated his beliefs that his cultural, legal, business relations with Latin America would help him in developing Arizona as a worthy competitor for Latin American trade. The next day, in "One Man's Opinion," by Bernie Wynn, Castro was described as "a fresh breeze over the Arizona political landscape, captivating Democrats and Republicans in his energetic bid for the governor's chair."

An *Arizona Republic* columnist, Walter W. Meek, wrote about the campaign:

"Stripped to its essentials, the governor's race is mainly a matter of personal credentials and whether the voters are in the mood for a change. It was only a small margin of voters who were not in the mood for change. The 1970 election was a very close loss because of slim margins in the rural Arizona counties. That year the Democratic party lost all of its races except one, the Secretary of State position won by Wesley Bolin. The 'cliff-hanger' gubernatorial race, therefore, showed Castro to be a very

**Governor Castro in his Office**
**Credit: Arizona Department of Library**
**Archives and Public Records**

significant challenger."

Wynn predicted that: We believe that Castro has a great future in the Democratic Party and should exercise his prerogative as titular leader to help rebuild Demo fortunes.

## CASTRO, THE GOVERNOR

Confirming Bernie Wynn's prediction that Castro had a great future role in the Democratic Party as "titular leader," Castro immediately began his 1974 campaign.

Castro's list of issues expanded for the 1974 campaign: 1) inflation; 2) air pollution; 3) land utilization; 4) law and order; 5) government dishonesty; and 6) women's rights.

To curb inflation, Castro pointed to the state's ever-expansive bureaucratic government, the productivity of state government employees, and Arizona's need for international, Latin American trade. First, a shift in policy or basic philosophy was needed to remedy a state budget rise from $425 million in 1971 to $735 million in 1974—a 75% increase in 4 years was an inflationary pattern that Castro took issue with. Second, state government employees' productivity would require application of basic, private enterprise system principles; or, a review of civil service rules to trim over-staffed offices or abolish unessential programs. Third, to boost international trade for Arizona, Castro recognized the need for Sky Harbor to become an international airport, for the University of Arizona and the Phoenix-based Arizona Heart Institute to attract patients from other countries where comparable facilities were not available, and for Arizona to develop economic relations with Mexico.

Castro caused controversy over some of his 1974 positions on certain issues. Some of his advocacies creating a stir included: a two-year deadline for the mining industry to reduce pollution, a severance tax on copper being shipped out of the state—which would NOT get his support—and withdrawal of public lands from mineral exploration. Asked to meet with mining leaders from the Arizona Mining Association and Phelps Dodge to explain his views of the industry's anti-pollution steps and tax contributions, he said, he was "not out to sink the mining industry in Arizona," for Arizona was a mining state and

"you don't kill the goose that laid the golden egg." As he elaborated and fielded questions, Mining Association President J. K. Richardson was satisfied with his "very fair, forthright" presentation.

There were other issues, of course, such as the energy crisis, judge's recall, plea bargaining, the two-party system, abortion, mandatory school redistricting, and the full disclosure law. In the 1974 campaign, Castro strongly believed that the next governor of Arizona should be: a governor with experience, ability, and leadership; a good judge, concerned with the rights of society and the constitutional rights of defendants, of victims' rights; and tough, to restore public confidence. Leadership experience, honesty and integrity were the main themes of the 1974 campaign whose slogan became "a choice for change." This time, the people made the choice for a change and Castro was elected Governor in 1974.

When Castro took over Arizona state government, it was a time of grim economic crisis. As pledged, he emphasized "no frills" budgeting and the Executive Budget was redone—$1 million less than the previous year, despite a 10 percent inflationary rate that year. He helped persuade President Gerald Ford to release impounded highway construction funds to re-invigorate the hard-hit construction industry. Known as a man of compassion and empathy, human resources received major emphasis with the creation of the Arizona Commission on the Status of Women and the Office of Affirmative Action. A special tribute was made to Arizona by constructing a state memorial to the *U.S.S. Arizona*, one of the ships sunk at Pearl Harbor on December 7, 1941. To promote trade, he provided new direction and leadership by establishing an Office of Tourism; reorganizing the Motion Picture Development; expanding the Four Corners Regional Commission to include all counties; creating the Border States Regional Commission to deal with U. S.—Mexico border problems; setting up a National and International Trade Commission to promote Arizona exports and foreign investments with the Far East, Europe, the Middle East, and Latin America.

## CASTRO, THE MAN

Castro personifies the self-made man. Bernie Wynn offering his "One Man's Opinion," in the October 16, 1970, *Arizona Republic*, and attributing the enormous respect that Castro was gaining from Democrats and Republicans to his "candid answers" to questions on where he stood on the issues, said, "Castro is no pussyfooter even when pussyfooting might be excused."

A Mexican-American whose cultural heritage lent "a color to his speech, a sparkle to his personality and a charm to his appeal," said Wynn, Castro was the underdog—a situation where, for one, everybody loves an underdog, and a situation reminiscent of his humble start in life that strengthened his determination to prosper despite the odds or the obstacles, and to relate to the needs of the working person, the underprivileged. Seeking "not love but respect," Castro was quoted to have said, Castro gained respect. Wynn's conclusion in 1970 was, "That's why we don't believe he can lose in the long run." In 1974, he did win, rising from humble beginnings to the governorship of Arizona.

Castro enjoys to relax by riding to a mountain top—for a "sense of humility." The Governor and his wife, Patricia Norris whom he married early in his career, in 1954, enjoyed their cabin in the woods, designed by the First Lady as a mountain-top retreat. For many years, they showed Shetland Hockney ponies throughout the United States. They operated the Castro Hockney Stables in Tucson. Another hobby is raising Irish wolfhounds which, in his dry wit, he once described as a "Mexican-Irish wolfhound . . . similar to an Irish wolfhound, only a little bit chubbier, with black wavy hair, a prominent nose and a well-manicured moustache." Pat and Raul have two daughters, Mary Pat and Beth, both married and living in California.

His love for Arizona and its people is evidenced by the many awards and honors bestowed him—by the Pima County Bar Association, the Daughters of American Revolution, the universities of Arizona, and other organizations. A special tribute—a park and recreation center—is dedicated to him in his native town of Cananea on behalf of the State of Sonora in Mexico.

A humble Hispanic, whose personal success story drew bipartisan support and whose underdog status was a "fresh" approach—one of honesty and integrity—Castro was described by a top ranking Democrat as "a reaffirmation of something that needs reaffirming these days, that a guy can make it on his own regardless of obstacles." In the 1970 campaign, said another Democrat, "had he mustered a surplus of 25,000 votes outside Maricopa, he would be a Messiah from the desert. But then Castro has been an uphill racer from the start." Both Arizona State University and Northern Arizona University have granted him Honorary Doctor's degrees. Universidad Autonoma de Guadalajara also awarded Governor Castro an Honorary Doctor's degree. In this case, as a prerequisite, he had to write a thesis or article to be placed in the University library.

In summing up his public service, one might do it with an acronym, which spells CASTRO:

Challenger,
Attorney,
Statesman,
Teacher,
Revolution's son
Overcomer of obstacles

## SOURCES

Goff, John S., *Arizona Biographical Dictionary*, Cave Creek, Arizona, Black Mountain Press, 1983, p. 107

Meek, Walter W., *Arizona Republic*, October 10, 1970

Pollack, Paul W., *Profiles of Prominent Personalities, (Arizona Edition)*, Phoenix, Arizona, Paul W. Pollock Published, 1977, p. 303

Wynn, Bernie, "One Man's Opinion," *Arizona Republic*, October 16, 1970

Wynn, Bernie, "One Man's Opinion," *Arizona Republic*, November 6, 1970

**Governor Harvey Wesley Bolin**
**Credit: Arizona Department of Library**
**Archives and Public Records**

# HARVEY WESLEY BOLIN

## 1977—1978

*Author: Dr. Robert Gryder*

Harvey Wesley Bolin was born in Butler, Missouri, on July 1, 1908. He and his family moved to Phoenix in 1917 at the end of World War I.

He graduated from Isaac School and Phoenix Union High School where he was a student leader. Young Wesley sold newspapers and caddied at the Country Club while attending Phoenix Union High School. He learned the dry cleaning business during the summer and after a semester at Phoenix College, he toured the country paying his expense by taking dry-cleaning jobs.

Fritz Marquardt made the following remarks about Governor Bolin.

"Wes could have been a Horatio Alger hero. He delivered the *Arizona Republic* in the morning, sold the *Phoenix Gazette* on a street corner in the afternoon, helped his father on the family farm out on West McDowell Road when he wasn't going to school.

"After he completed his studies at Phoenix Junior College he entered the dry cleaning business. After working in that business for some time, he lived both in Chicago and Salt Lake City but he returned to Phoenix in 1935."

After he returned to Phoenix from several years of touring the country, he joined the Young Democrats, pressed party leaders, and in 1938 was elected to his first political office—Constable of the West Phoenix Justice Precinct. He served until 1942, when he was appointed West Phoenix Justice of the Peace. While in that political office, Bolin and Tucson Justice of the Peace Jack Gardner organized the Arizona Justices of the Peace and Constables Association. Bolin served as its first secretary-treasurer.

From the years 1939-1942, he served as constable of the West Phoenix Precinct Justice Court. Later he was appointed Justice

of the Peace for an unexpired term. He was re-elected every two years until 1948. During these years he was studying law through correspondence school courses. The Secretary of State position was vacated when Dan Garvey succeeded the dying Governor Sidney P. Osborn. Bolin decided to bid for it, as did many others.

In 1948, Wesley became a candidate for the Democratic nomination for the Arizona Secretary of State. He won in the primary and general elections and assumed office in January, 1949. Even though Wesley Bolin was opposed by five well-known contenders for the position as Secretary of State, Bolin surprised the pundits by winning the primary with a 10,000 vote margin. He went on to win the general election by an overwhelming 50,000 votes.

Bolin was continually re-elected time after time and served in that capacity for almost thirty years. During this long period of time, he was frequently acting governor when a chief executive was absent from the State of Arizona. Wesley Bolin served as Chairman of the Code Commission which revised the Arizona statutes in 1956.

As Secretary of State, Bolin was busy as the state's official greeter for foreign visitors, celebrities, business leaders and government officials. He continued to be re-elected Secretary of State every two years. During those years rarely did any candidate choose to oppose the popular Secretary of State.

Wesley Bolin was a large, handsome, friendly man who was well-liked throughout the State of Arizona. Bolin, a Democrat, was equally at home in the Republican camp. His ability to work cooperatively with both political parties is a credit to his foresight and is an example of his leadership in working with all

**Governor Wesley Bolin at the State of Arizona Legislature**
**Credit: Arizona Department of Library**
**Archives and Public Records**

**Governor Bolin Presenting a Proclamation to
Arizona Students
Credit: Arizona Department of Library
Archives and Public Records**

citizens of the state.

In 1953, Wesley Bolin was elected President of the National Association of Secretaries of State. He continued to be an active leader in that organization for many years. In 1956, he was chairman of the Arizona Code Commission, which hammered out the Arizona Revised Statutes that year. The codes produced were a major milestone in Arizona law.

Wesley Bolin was recognized for his active involvement in numerous community affairs. He was a ready sponsor of charitable efforts, was a Boy Scout leader, and received the Silver Beaver and Silver Antelope from the Roosevelt Council in Phoenix. He was a sincere champion of Arizona's growing number of disadvantaged citizens. As an avid horseman he was a frequent and popular rider in scores of rodeo parades held in the State of Arizona. Always a political advisor, his sage counsel was sought by men and women in both political parties.

Conservative by nature and combined with a self-effacing personality, Wesley Bolin won thousands of friends in Arizona—and in the nation as well. It has been written that "few men understood the workings of Arizona government as well as he, and few served his state longer and more effectively."

The fifteenth state governor of Arizona served from October 20, 1977, from the resignation of Governor Raul Castro, until his untimely death on March 4, 1978. The man who inherited the Arizona governor's office when Raul Castro became ambassador to Argentina was no stranger to that job.

Bolin had served as Secretary of State for 28 years under 7 of Arizona's 14 governors. No one has held a single state-wide office longer than Bolin, who also has become acting governor whenever a chief executive left the state. Bolin also attributed his long career to a tendency to "mind my own business" and "never interfere in any other state department."

The First Lady of the Bolin administration was Mrs. Marion Knappenberger Bolin, his second wife. Everyone in Phoenix seemed to know Wes Bolin, who had been Secretary of State for years and had as many friends in the Republican party as he did in his own Democratic group. Fewer people knew his wife Marion. What kind of First Lady would

she be? That's the question asked people who knew her as Mrs. Moulton Knappenberger, wife of a cotton rancher who died in 1966—or an active member of Central Methodist Church—or as a dedicated worker for Boy Scouts or the Navy League. The answer was "gracious." But then there were other equally kind adjectives.

Mrs. Charles R. Bell, first president of Arizona Cotton Wives: "I've known Marion for 15 years and she is such a gracious person and such a hard worker. She enjoys tackling any kind of project and carrying it through, but she prefers to work behind the scenes without recognition. She is very creative and her home reflects her creativeness. She also showed managerial qualities when she took over management of her former husband's ranch and remained in agriculture for many years."

Wes Bolin was far more than a glad-hander. He attended the first year in a junior college, however, he took correspondence courses in law. He knew more about legal procedures than many members of the Bar.

Fritz Marquardt frequently sought his opinion on some tricky legal question and he invariably reached for the Arizona Revised Statutes to settle the matter. Wesley Bolin was chairman of the commission which made the 1956 revision of that book.

According to Marquardt, Wes Bolin could be called the last of the Pintos.

Columbus Giragi, an Arizona publisher with great political savvy, coined the word to describe an Arizona politician who had his foot in both the Democratic and the Republican party camps. It also was used to describe a conservative Democrat.

To most people it's a perjorative word. But Giragi didn't think of it that way. He called himself a Pinto. His slogan was, "Vote for the man, not the party."

Whether a Republican or a Democrat was in office made no difference to Bolin. He worked smoothly with both and has been called for counsel and aid by Republican governors almost as readily as by those of the Democratic party.

Marquardt continued to write that even though Bolin was often urged to run for governor, he was never assured of enough Democrat support to make the primary race worthwhile. He preferred to remain Secretary of State, where for 28 years he was unbeatable.

Bolin worked so well with Republicans that, on at least one occasion, they ran no one against him.

Bolin's finest quality was his concern for his fellow citizens. He probably knew more people by name than anyone else in the state. He started learning names and faces when he traveled the state for his dry-cleaning business. He kept it up during his 28 years as Secretary of State, a period during which he cut ribbons and ate chicken lunches nearly every day.

Governor Wesley Bolin, 68, died in his home about 3 a.m. on March 4, 1978, of an apparent heart attack. The Governor had served just over four months as the state's chief executive.

Jack Swanson, writing in the *Arizona Republic* stated that "he was plain-spoken and down-to-earth. He loved people and Arizona." "I can think of no better way than this by which to remember our friend Wesley Bolin," remarked the Reverend Dr. Culver H. Nelson. "It is no euphemism to say of him 'He was a public servant!'" "Wes died doing what he loved to do: help others."

Nelson also commented that Governor Bolin was less concerned for ideology than people. "When most were conversing about civil rights, he was putting blacks to work as summer interns. When equal opportunity for women was mostly committee work, he was appointing them to high places on his staff and encouraging this everywhere."

John Kolbe added that "People and this 'great state of Arizona' (one word, in the Bolin vocabulary) were the passions of his long and well-spent life. They were not to be used, but nurtured and cultivated and cherished as friends." He continued to say "That people were also voters, the stuff of politics, seemed almost beside the point. He did not make friends because he was in politics; he was in politics because it was the best way to meet a lot of people."

Kolbe added that Bolin "as an involuntary refugee from a simpler era, that was enough." He won 13 consecutive terms as Secretary of State (probably spending, in all 13 campaigns, about as much as a sheriff's campaign costs today (1978) by simply being Wes Bolin—the incomparable ribbon-snipper, parade marshal, convention welcomer, award presenter, hand shaker, lady kisser and unfailingly consummate gentleman.

"Big-time politics now is a dizzying plethora of sophisticated polls, expensive consultants, slick advertising and scientific fund-raising techniques which were foreign to Bolin. His opponents have them—he didn't. He remained confident, to the end, the warm smile and that bone-wrenching handshake would come through again."

President Jimmy Carter and his wife Rosalyn extended their sympathy to Bolin's widow and to the people of Arizona. The President recalled Bolin's trip last week to the National Governors' Conference in Washington. "He dined with us at the White House and danced with Rosalyn to begin the evening's entertainment," the President said. "We join the many others who knew the warmth of his personality and are saddened by his death."

Arizona Secretary of State Rose Mofford's voice broke when she commented on the end of her 22-year friendship with Bolin. "It's the worst shock I ever had," she said. "It was just like losing my brother. He was a fine person."

Ernest McFarland, 82, former Governor, Arizona Supreme Court Chief Justice and U.S. Senator, said of Bolin, "He was honest and performed many services for his state and the people."

Paul Fannin, former U.S. Senator and Arizona Governor, called Bolin "One of the most dedicated office-holders I have ever had the privilege to work with."

Phoenix Mayor Margaret Hance, in Washington for a U.S. League of Cities meeting said, "I talked to the Governor last night and the memory is still vivid in my mind. I will miss him, his many friends will miss him and the people of Arizona will miss him."

Carolyn Warner, State Superintendent of Public Instruction, said, "I honor Wes Bolin. I honor his life for what it meant to the people of this state. I honor his memory because it will live on to remind us all of the true meaning of the words 'public service.'"

Scottsdale Mayor William C. Jenkins said Bolin "established a long and enviable record of service to the people of Arizona."

Henry Haws, Vice Chairman of the Maricopa Board of Supervisors, commented, "We have lost a good public servant."

Mary Lobel, Phoenix Coordinator for

**Governor Bolin— "Punching It Out"**
**Credit: Arizona Department of Library**
**Archives and Public Records**

the Arizona Women's Political Caucus extended her group's condolences to Bolin's family.

Simpson Cox, a Phoenix lawyer and longtime friend of Bolin said "Thousands of people will miss him." "Wes cared for humanity," Cox said. "But, more than that, he recognized and had concern for each individual with whom he became acquainted."

## SOURCES

Boyles, Lois, "Governor Bolin Dies," *Phoenix Gazette*, March 4, 1978

"Capitol Plaza Formally Named After Wes Bolin," *Phoenix Gazette*, March 8, 1978

Goff, John S., *Arizona Biographical Dictionary*, Black Mountain Press, Cave Creek, Arizona, 1983, p 13

"Governor Bolin Dies at 69," *Arizona Republic*, March 5, 1978

Kolbe, John, "Wesley Bolin Finally Gets 'Big Chance'" *Phoenix Gazette*, August 19, 1977

Kolbe, John, "People-Loving Wes Bolin Set Memorable Example,"*Phoenix Gazette*, March 6, 1978

Leckey, Andy, "Arizonans Pay Last Respects to Wes Bolin,"*Phoenix Gazette*, March 6, 1978

*History of Arizona, Volume III*, Lewis Historical Publishing Company, Inc., New York, 1958, p. 55

Marquadt, Fritz, "State Bids Farewell To Its No.1 Public Servant," *Arizona Republic,* March 5, 1978

Moore, Art, "Wesley Bolin: The State Was His Family," *Phoenix Gazette*, March 7, 1978

*Arizona's Men of Achievement, Volume I,* Paul W. Pollock Publishers, Phoenix, Arizona, 1958, p. 294

*Arizona Biographical Encyclopedia, Volume III*, Paul W. Pollock Publishers, Phoenix, Arizona, 1981, p. 275

Swanson, Jack, "Requiem for the 'Servant of All'—1,000 Mourn at Bolin Funeral," *Arizona Republic,* March 8, 1978

"Wesley Bolin—40 years of Dedication to Arizona," *Phoenix Gazette*, March 4, 1978

Zipf, Walter, "Wes Bolin Man of Friendships,"*Sun Valley Spur-*

*Shopper*, October 6, 1977

**Governor Bruce Babbitt**
**Credit: Arizona Department of Library**
**Archives and Public Records**

# BRUCE BABBITT

## 1978—1987

*Author: Dr. Donald J. Tate*

An early morning telephone call on March 4, 1978, dramatically jolted Attorney General Bruce Babbitt into an "undreamed dream-come-true reality"—Arizona's sixteenth and youngest governor (age 39).

The right of succession, according to the Arizona constitution, had suddenly taken another step. Governor Raul Castro resigned in 1977; Secretary of State Wesley Bolin was heart stricken six months later; Attorney General Bruce Babbitt was elevated to new responsibilities. Another chapter in the history of Arizona had opened.

Who was this young Attorney General, who by fate was thrust into the office of Arizona's chief executive?

This young public figure disappointed many of his champions in 1976 when he ran again for Attorney General and was re-elected. They had wanted him to run for governor that year because of his potency as a vote getter in 1974. Of course, speculations about his running for governor for a full term surfaced almost instantly when he succeeded Wesley Bolin. Run successfully he did in 1978 and again in 1982.

As he started his second full term, some praised him as a rising political star; others described him as a man in a hurry. Obviously, he pleased some citizens of Arizona and displeased others, yet he wasted no time in agonizing over such reality.

Jack Brown, Babbitt's former boss and legal mentor, described him as "extremely bright and energetic, shrewd and tough." Even critics of Bruce Babbitt paid him compliments. For example, John Kolbe stated that "Babbitt is a man of considerable intelligence, wit, vision and many other talents." Individuals from quite different walks of life pointed out many desirable traits marking his character.

Bruce's mother, Frances Babbitt, added to these traits when she said he accomplished so much through "Hard work, dedication and discipline . . . "

Insight into who Bruce Babbitt, a third generation Arizonan, is and why his life unfolded as it has, can be drawn by overviewing the life and adventures of his family, starting with Grandfather Charles Babbitt and his brothers.

The lure of the West captured the imagination of the Babbitt brothers. Tales of fortunes made "out there" were heard in Cincinnati, where David Babbitt opened a grocery store in 1882. One brother went West in 1884 to scout for a place to settle. He looked at Kansas, Colorado and Wyoming before moving on to the the territories of New Mexico and Arizona. From Tucson, his enthusiastic reports were cautiously evaluated before the Babbitts boarded a train on February 25, 1886.

By chance they were persuaded to go to Flagstaff after arriving in Albuquerque. Within a month they had bought several head of cattle. The brothers acquired more range land and water sources to accommodate large herds. The cattle business did well, and thoughts of business opportunities in town followed. The Flagstaff store attracted ranchers and Indian traders from a wide area. Cash, Navajo rugs, wood, hides, or cattle were used to purchase goods. Credit was offered and accepted. Soon the Babbitts were serving as Flagstaff's bank. In 1888, the Citizen's Bank was launched, David Babbitt being one of the partners.

Ed, the youngest brother, graduated from law school "back East." Before returning to Cincinnati to practice law, he had served as a probate judge and as a member of the Arizona Territorial Council. The earlier Babbitts extended their business interests to public service.

**Governor Bruce Babbitt**
**1983 Inauguration**
**Credit: Department of Library**
**Archives and Public Records**

**Governor Bruce Babbitt**
**Credit: The Phoenix Newspapers, Inc.**

Challenges were commonplace in the lives of these early Babbitts. Not knowing about the nature of a wide array of businesses did not deter them from operating Flagstaff's "opera house," ice plant, livery stable, mortuary and meat packing plant. Also, they "learned on the job" as they became involved in real estate, a hotel, and automobile dealerships.

These entrepreneurs overcame adversities of the post war recession and the 1932 depression. Later Babbitts restructured the enterprises suffering from economic reversals—these younger Babbitts looked forward just as their predecessors had.

Into this pioneering, venturesome, visionary, successful family, Bruce E. Babbitt was born June 27, 1938—too soon to profit from World War II experiences but in time to witness and experience the 1950s rock-n'-roll decade and the activism of the 1960s.

If test scores, school grades, and class presidencies are valid indicators of success, Bruce Babbitt was destined to be an achiever in later life just as he was in elementary and high school. Seemingly, his agile mind shaped his future and guided him to the gates of opportunity.

Parental guidance during these formative years demanded discipline and strongly encouraged participation in activities outside the classroom. Summer jobs were a part of the plan. Bruce's mother believed every child in the family should be able to play an instrument and to sing. She had played in the Los Angeles Philharmonic; in Flagstaff she helped establish the local symphony. Bruce's father was more successful in nurturing an interest in nature than his mother was in fostering musicianship. His father, an amateur anthropologist, often took his young children rock and ruin hunting. The foundations of an interest in geology were laid for Bruce.

From Flagstaff Bruce went to the University of Notre Dame where he earned a B. A. degree with a major in geology. He graduated Magna Cum Laude and served a term as student body president, a record much like his high school achievements. In 1963, he was awarded a master's degree in geophysics at the University of Newcastle, England, his master's thesis being a study of volcanic geology in the Grand Canyon, Arizona region.

While studying geophysics in England, he and his classmates would fly off to Paraguay and Bolivia, where they analyzed a phenomenon known as "continental drift." Oil company research crews helicoptered Babbitt and others to and from the Andes Mountains, where the students would measure the land actually moving. On these trips, Babbitt was struck by the contrast between the opulence of the oil companies and the poverty of the countrymen.

This broadening experience deepened his thinking about people and dying infants because he had seen first-hand the poverty and misery in Andean countries. His background in science was to become knowledge for future use, not a fulfillment of boyhood dreams about a career.

His final years in a structured educational environment began with enrollment in the Harvard Law School. His law degree was granted in 1965. Later in the year he was admitted to the Arizona Bar, although he did not practice law at that time.

Informal education has been important to Bruce Babbitt. He has been studying Arizona History for many years, much of it carried on by him unknowingly as a boy. No doubt his interest was whetted merely by being surrounded by a family who really made history.

Concrete results of Bruce Babbitt's interest in Arizona history can be found in two books, one being the *Grand Canyon an anthology*. Robert C. Euler in the foreword of the book wrote, "Now, for the first time many writings, selected from the not more than thirty falling into an enduring category, have been brought together . . . by a person who . . . has long carried on a literary love affair with Grand Canyon."

Another statement by Robert C. Euler, "sciences, law, geology and the humanities, couple that with his long interest in all facets of *Grand Canyon,* including backpacking and river running, and his expertise becomes clear."

The second book by Bruce Babbitt, *Color and Light, The Southwest Canvas of Louis Akin* reveals his understanding and appreciation of Southwestern art. Clay Lockett in the foreword notes that the works of Akin and some of his contemporaries constituted the beginning of regional art in Arizona. Lockett stated "this book is a belated, but well-deserved recognition for one of the first serious artists to

**Governor Babbitt
Enjoying his Bike Ride
Credit: The Phoenix Newspapers, Inc.**

live in Arizona . . . ."

From Harvard Bruce Babbitt went to the U. S. Office of Economic Opportunity as a Special Assistant to the Director of VISTA, an anti-poverty program. He was responsible for promoting community action programs. In this job he broadened his background in basic people problems. In the Spring of 1965, he was in Selma, Alabama, where he had a direct experience in social activism as he participated in the Civil Rights Movement.

From 1967 until he took office as Attorney General of Arizona, he was a partner in a Phoenix law firm.

During these years he was an attorney for the Navajo Tribe. In this capacity he won the 1972 reapportionment case which ended the gerrymandering of legislative districts on the Navajo reservation. This legislation resulted in Indians serving in the legislature.

Other involvement in matters of special concern to Arizonans were his serving as counsel for the Arizona Wildlife Federation and the Arizona Newspaper Association. He participated in drafting a bill requiring public agencies to open their meetings to the public when he served as counsel for the newspaper organization. Believing all people need adequate legal services, he was active in the Maricopa Legal Aid Society.

In general, these activities provided Bruce Babbitt the opportunity to continue his social activities. During these years as he practiced law and worked on special "people" problems, problems which he earnestly believed had to be seriously addressed. Arizona faced problems of land fraud and public corruption.

The years 1967-1974 enabled Bruce Babbitt to observe Arizona's government, its business climate, and its citizens. His nearly three years as Attorney General were a time when he shaped changes in law enforcement.

Two recognized thrusts during Babbitt's term as Attorney General from 1975-1978 were "an immense broadening of the Attorney General's power to bring criminal charges" (which prior to Babbitt was limited to county attorneys) and the enforcing of "antitrust laws that had been on the books for decades but never used."

"Had Bruce Babbitt never become governor, he still would have been remembered as the best Attorney General Arizona ever had,"

according to those who worked for Babbitt during these notable years.

What was his legacy of serving as governor for nearly nine years, 1978-1987? An elevation of awareness of state government and a depth of discussion of governance may be the most important aspect of Bruce Babbitt's legacy to Arizona. The thickness of files of newspaper clippings in libraries attests to this observation. A veritable avalanche of print on Bruce Babbitt, issues, political personages, debates, his family, his ancestors, rolled from the presses. Challenging the *status quo* in governance provoked debate and partisan comment, but changes did come about.

Governor Babbitt himself articulated much of the legacy contained in columns by political pundits. Don Harris in the *Arizona Republic* reported the salient points as he thought them to be:

A vastly different, much stronger (governor's) office.

Arizonans' expectations, are that they will have a governor who governs.

The landmark 1980 Act designed to protect Arizona's groundwater supply.

The unfinished business of remedying county governments still operating under nineteenth century rules and procedures.

Using the veto, a record of 114 times, forcing lawmakers to deal with issues.

The states answer to Medicaid—the Arizona Health Care Cost Containment System.

Mending the rift between Labor and the Democratic party after the Phelps Dodge strikes in Clifton-Morenci.

Demonstrating to the legislature that a governor can set the legislative agenda.

In shaping this legacy, part of which often evolved after heated debate in the legislature and exchange of words by friends and critics ranging from vitriolic to praiseworthy, Bruce Babbitt professionalized Arizona's state government.

Bruce Babbitt's leaving the governor's office after occupying it for 8 3/4 years, closed a chapter of Arizona history. Additional chapters could be written on his relationships with his family—wife Hattie and two sons—and his seeking the candidacy of President of the United States. Also, analytical treatises could be written on his political life while serving the State of Arizona. In the meantime,

Arizonans can remember one of the best educated governors Arizona has had.

## SOURCES

*Arizona Republic,* December 28, 1988

Babbitt, Bruce, *Color and Light, The Southwest Convasses of Louis Akin,* Northland Press, Flagstaff, Arizona, 1973

Babbitt, Bruce, *Grand Canyon,* Northland Press, Flagstaff, Arizona, 1978

"Biography of Bruce E. Babbitt, Governor of Arizona," Unpublished

Goff, John S., *Arizona Biographical Dictionary,* Black Mountain Press, Cave Creek, Arizona, 1983

Mofford, Mary, "The First Family," *Arizona Living,* March, 1978

*Peoples Weekly*, Vol. 12, No. 26, December, 1979

*Phoenix Gazette*, November 2, 1978

*Phoenix Gazette*, December 26, 1986

Pollack, Paul W., *Arizona Biographical Encyclopedia*, Phoenix, Arizona, 1981

*Who's Who in Arizona*, Success Publishing Company, Scottsdale, Arizona, 1984

Yack, Patrick, *Empire Magazine, The Denver Post,* April 14, 1985

**Governor Evan Mecham**
**Credit: Arizona Department of Library**
**Archives and Public Records**

# EVAN MECHAM

## 1987—1988

*Author: Dr. Marianne M. Jennings*

Like many successful business people of his era, Evan Mecham came from humble beginnings. He was born on May 12, 1924, in Duchesne, Utah. His early childhood taught him the value of hard work and persistence; the two qualities that would earn him the state's highest elected office. Following his graduation from Altamont High School in Duchesne, he received an agricultural scholarship to Utah State University. He attended Utah State from 1942-43 and then left to become an Army Air Force pilot in the country's battle in Europe during World War II.

It was during his active duty in World War II that the evidence of his strength under pressure became evident. He flew fighter planes out of England and was awarded the Air Medal and Purple Heart. For a time during the war he was a prisoner of war in Germany.

Following his military service, young Mecham returned to Arizona to continue his college studies. He attended Arizona State University from 1947 to 1950 majoring in management and economics. Three years later, in 1950, and 16 credit hours short of a degree, Evan Mecham opened Mecham Pontiac and Rambler in Ajo. In 1954, he moved the dealership to what was then the outskirts of Phoenix — the Glendale area. The initial car business grew into several other family-owned businesses including Mecham Racing, Hauahaupan Mining Company and several dealerships in other states. Mr. Mecham served as President and Chairman of the Board of Mecham Pontiac until the dealership was sold in 1988.

In addition to the tremendous energy devoted to his business, which would eventually put him in the category of self-made millionaires, Evan Mecham was busy with family and church responsibilities. It was during these early years that he married his wife, Florence, and together their family would grow to include four sons and three daughters. Those children have all married and as of 1989, Governor and Mrs. Mecham were grandparents of eighteen grandchildren. Governor Mecham and his family are very active in their church, the Church of Jesus Christ of Latter Day Saints, more commonly known as the "Mormons," and Evan Mecham held several positions of responsibility in the church including bishop and stake leadership positions.

It was very early in his business career that Mecham developed an interest in the political arena and in 1960 he held his first elected office with a two-year term in the Arizona State Senate. During his tenure in office he became widely known because of his committed and unwavering expressions of his conservative views. Many have said that Evan Mecham's conservatism may be his worst foe.

At the end of his short senate service, Mecham ran for the Republican party's nomination for the U.S. Senate seat held by then-incumbent Senator Carl Hayden. He won the 1962 GOP nomination for the seat at a time when the John Birch Society enjoyed tremendous popularity in the Phoenix area. Evan Mecham was described as "scrappy" in his campaign against the institution of the then 85-year-old Senator Hayden. During the race, Mr. Mecham received the endorsement of the *Tucson Daily Citizen* but Mr. Hayden won re-election and then retired after that final sixth term in the U. S. Senate.

Mecham was concerned about the lack of support from his Republican party during this Senate race and ran for state chairman in 1963 but was defeated by Keith Brown. In spite of the defeat, Evan Mecham remained active in party government and supported

**Governor Mecham**
**Delivering a Speech**
**Credit: The Phoenix Newspapers, Inc.**

Charles Miller in his successful run for Maricopa County chairman of the Republican party. During Mr. Miller's chairmanship, the county party committee experienced division into two ideological camps with Mecham and Miller on one side and moderate Republicans on the other. After a $20,000 loss, Senator Barry Goldwater stepped into local party activities and led a reform movement that subsequently restored party unity. The dispute later proved to be a scenario that would be repeated following Mecham's impeachment. It was also during this time (1963-1973) that he published his own newspaper, *American,* a newspaper known for its conservative views and challenges to current business and political leaders.

In 1964, Evan Mecham made his first of five runs for the Governor of Arizona. While often labeled the Harold Stassen of Arizona, his persistence brought him back until he won the coveted Governor's seat in 1986. In that first 1964 election he was defeated in the primary by Richard Kleindienst, who would lose the election but later become the U. S. Attorney General under Richard Nixon. He ran again in 1974 and 1982 with his high point in 1978 when he won 46 percent of the popular vote in an election in which his opponent was Bruce Babbitt, a newly appointed incumbent who was re-elected to the office in 1982. During the twelve-year period between 1974 and 1986, the Democrats held the Governor's seat until eventually Mecham would win back the state house for the Republican party in 1986.

The 1986 election was comprised of a series of strange events that would pave the way for Mecham's victory. As late as June of 1986, he was still undecided about entering the race for a fifth time but was eventually convinced to enter the race after a demonstration of widespread support for his campaign. In the primary campaign, Mecham ran against the then speaker of the Arizona House—Burton Barr. His candidacy was greeted as one of the perennial loser and virtually disregarded. Mecham's message, however, struck a nerve with voters as he geared his campaign to "the guy who has to brown-bag it when he goes to work," and he developed a strong following with his indictments of the business and political "insiders."

"Certain members of the ruling establishment are always using their positions, wealth and influence to elect people in both parties to do their bidding. Thus they are not concerned with what party is in power as long as the party member wielding that power is holding [sic] to them on the key issues that us the government powers for their own gain."

In an intense primary campaign that was labeled as "mud slinging" and caused former Senate president Stan Turley to label an "ethical pygmy," Mecham, to the surprise of party leadership, captured the nomination. However, it was perhaps what happened on the Democratic side that resulted in Evan Mecham's victory in the general election. Carolyn Warner was the Democrat's nominee for the office following the withdrawal of William Schultz from the race due to a family illness. After the conclusion of the primaries and well into Mrs. Warner's and Mr. Mecham's campaign, Mr. Schultz announced that he would return to the race as an independent candidate and he easily collected the signatures necessary for such a run. The vote-split between these two Democrats allowed Mecham to win the Governor's seat without a majority vote but simply more votes than the other two. Evan Mecham, the surprising perennial candidate emerged victorious in his fifth, but not final run.

Shortly after his victory, the description of himself that Mr. Mecham used on his billboard in his 1962 run against Senator Carl Hayden became a motto, "You know where he stands." Mecham took a number of definite and controversial stands and was once described by his press secretary, Ken Smith, as follows: "The governor has a tendency to put his foot in his mouth." His first official act was to repeal the controversial Martin Luther King Jr. holiday that had been declared by the outgoing Bruce Babbitt. The public outcry and debate on the holiday would continue long after Governor Mecham would leave office. His first few months in office witnessed additional and continued controversy as questionable appointments were made and some charges of insensitivity to women and minorities were made. Some highlights of the controversies included his nomination for director of revenue a man whose company was $25,000 in arrears on employment compensation payments; his defense of the use of the word "pickaninny" in

**Governor Evan Mecham**
**"Making his Point"**
**Credit: The Phoenix Newspapers, Inc.**

a book he had advocated as a term of affection; his cancellation his newspaper subscription for the newspaper's description of Florence's clothes as "cheap" and "garish," and his threats to banish reporters from press conferences and a nationally known statement to a reporter, "Don't you ever ask me for a true statement again."

By the end of his first six months in office, Governor Mecham was the focus of what would prove to be a successful recall drive. The Mecham for Ex-Governor campaign headed by Phoenix businessman Ed Buck resulted in an ugly and emotionally-charged political climate. When notified of the recall election, Governor Mecham stated:

"In fact, I would welcome a recall election—next week, next month. At least a recall election I think would shut 'em all up. I'll tell you what, if a band of homosexuals and a few dissident Democrats can get me out of office, why heavens, the state deserves what else they can get."

The recall movement gained further momentum when a reporter for the *Arizona Republic* disclosed the existence of a controversial issue in Mecham's campaign finances; the so-called $350,000 "Wolfson loan" which was not specifically disclosed in his campaign disclosure filings. The reporter for the *Arizona Republic*, Sam Stanton, had obtained a copy of a letter from Governor Mecham to developer Barry Wolfson in which Mecham promised to keep the loan confidential. Yet another controversy surfaced when Mecham used funds raised at his inaugural ball for a loan to his Mecham Pontiac business after an investigation by the county attorney determined that the funds raised had been in violation of Arizona campaign finance laws and that the funds could not be used to repay campaign debts but must be placed in trust for use for public purposes. A final controversy that would contribute to Governor Mecham's impeachment was a charge of his interference in the investigation of a threat made by one of his employees to another employee of state government.

While the controversies swirled, the recall movement proved to be a success with a total of 343,913 signatures collected. The signatures were delivered to the Secretary of State, Rose Mofford, and Mrs. Mofford validated the signatures on February 8, 1988,

and scheduled a recall election for May 17, 1988.

The recall movement proved to be but one-third of the difficulties Governor Mecham would face. It was late in 1987, when then-House Speaker Joe Lane hired an attorney for the House to begin the process of investigating Governor Mecham's actions with respect to the loan, the inaugural funds and the threat to determine whether impeachable offenses had occurred. The final third of Governor Mecham's difficulties came between the time the special counsel was hired and the report recommending impeachment was issued, when Arizona Attorney General Bob Corbin secured a state grand jury indictment of Governor Mecham and his brother Willard for perjury, willful concealment and filing false reports in connection with the Wolfson loan.

When special House counsel William French submitted his report to the House, his recommendation was that impeachable offenses had occurred and that impeachment hearings should proceed.

In spite of the difficulties, Governor Mecham stood firm in his resolve to remain in office, prepared for the legislative session, and, in his state-of-the-state address, he was conciliatory and acknowledged that he had "made mistakes." The speech, however, preceded Mr. French's report and four days after Governor Mecham's address, the House Select committee was formed to conduct impeachment hearings. Testimony in the impeachment hearing began on January 19, 1988, with Governor Mecham testifying at the end of those hearings for two days. On February 5, 1988, the House voted (46-14) to impeach and the case was referred to the Arizona Senate for trial.

The Senate trial began in February with Chief Justice Frank Gordon presiding. During the time of the Senate trial, Mr. Mecham was no longer Governor since the vote of impeachment had the result of removal from office and Rose Mofford, the then Secretary of State, assumed the Governorship. The proceedings in the criminal charges ran out simultaneously with the Mechams' arraignment occurring shortly after Governor Mecham's impeachment.

After a Senate trial that lasted five weeks and found most Arizonans tuned in to the proceedings or the night replays of them, the Senate voted to impeach Governor Mecham. Following his permanent removal from office, the trial on the criminal charges was held and Mecham and his brother Willard were acquitted.

In the impeachment findings, the Senate did not invoke what has been called the "Dracula" clause which would have prohibited Mr. Mecham from ever again holding public office. As a result, Mr. Mecham spent most of 1988 bolstering support and announced his sixth run for the governor's seat in 1989. In addition, Mr. Mecham became a formidable figure in the Republican party organization, winning election as a delegate to the national convention in 1988 and successfully working to unseat many of the legislators who voted to impeach him. His participation in the legislative elections, under a campaign labeled, "Come November, we'll remember," resulted in upsets in House and Senate leadership and composition and his influence continues to be felt through the supporters who were elected and the reluctance of others to risk opposition of the former Governor's supporters.

While his time in office was short and marked by significant controversy, Mr. Mecham remains a force in the Arizona political arena and emerges as the Governor who brought not only significant national attention to Arizona but also brought many citizens lessons in the functions and roles of the various branches of government. Mr. Mecham's announcement of his candidacy for 1990 is consistent with his lifetime quality of persistence in pursuit of a goal that may yet be fulfilled.

## SOURCES

*Arizona Republic*—April 19, 1974, B1,
    August 5, 1974, B1,
    September 3, 1974, A1,
    September 4, 1974, A1,
    September 5, 1974, B1,
    July 2, 1986,
    October 9, 1986, E1,
    October 10, 1986, A4,
    January 9, 1988, A1,
    February 6, 1988, A1,
    April 14, 1988, A1
Personal letter, Senatorial Campaign, October
    10, 1962
*Phoenix Gazette*—May 28, 1986, B1,

    June 11, 1986, B3,
    July 2, 1986, B2,
    January 9, 1988, A1,
    January 11, 1988, A1
*Human Events,* October 20, 1962, p.1
*Tucson Daily Citizen*, October 11, 1962
*People Magazine*, October 1987 p. 39
*San Francisco Examiner,* November 22, 1987,
    E1
*Mesa Tribune,* October 14, 1986, A1

**Governor Rose P. Mofford**
**Credit: Arizona Department of Library**
**Archives and Public Records**

# ROSE MOFFORD

## 1988—1990

*Author: Dr. Marianne M. Jennings*

Rose Mofford is unique in that she is Arizona's first female chief executive. More than that, she is probably the first governor to have a listed home phone number and return all the calls she receives. Such dedication is perhaps the product of the strong work ethic of her rural Arizona upbringing. She was born Rose Perica on June 10, 1922, in Globe, Arizona. She was the youngest of six children born to John and Frances Perica. Their residence in Six Shooter Canyon was a training ground for the value of discipline and hard work that would see her through the challenges ahead. The strong influence of her Austrian immigrant parents' pride in their country and state would prompt Rose into a career in public service spanning half a century.

Her school work was outstanding and she was the first female class president at Globe High School. She graduated in 1939 not only as valedictorian but with the highest grade average ever earned at Globe High. She had a great interest in athletics and played softball and basketball. At one time, at her father's insistence, she gave up the chance to play professional basketball with a team known as the All-American Redheads—given her famous snow white hair, she probably chose the correct career path.

Upon graduation from high school, she began her work in state government in 1940 and during that time dealt personally with 12 of Arizona's 16 governors. After arriving at the state capitol, she took on various assignments. Her first job, at the age of 17, was as a secretary to Joe Hunt, who was then the state treasurer. When Hunt was elected to the Tax Commission, Rose Perica followed and remained with the Tax Commission until 1945 when she left for a year to become the business manager for Arizona Highways. She returned to the Tax Commission as an executive secretary and remained for another 13 years through Hunt's retirement in 1950 when she was fired by Commissioner Thad Moore who indicated he wanted a man to fill the position. Governor Mofford describes the incident as Mr. Moore giving her "the opportunity to step down."

In the midst of her stint at the Tax Commission, Rose Perica became Rose Mofford when she married T. R. "Lefty" Mofford in 1957. Mr. Mofford, who was then the deputy state treasurer, had been a founding officer of the Phoenix Police Department. He later became an adult probation officer for Maricopa County and finished his public service career as assistant securities director for the Arizona Corporation Commission. During their ten-year marriage, the Moffords tried unsuccessfully to adopt children and opened their home to foster children and students who needed some place to stay until they got started in school or found employment. Their home was always full of young people who stayed anywhere from three to six months under this unique Mofford program that preceded all the work for the homeless that would later be part of the work of Governor Mofford's administration. The Moffords were later divorced but remained friends with Rose caring for Lefty during his last illness and personally paying his medical bills.

After her dismissal from the Tax Commission, Rose left for the secretary of state's office and stayed 22 years. In 1975, because of what she believed was a career slump, she left the office to become assistant director of the State Revenue Department (previously the Tax Commission). However, in October of 1977, then-Governor Raul Castro was appointed U. S. Ambassador to Argentina and Wesley Bolin became governor. In spite of her years of service as assistant secretary of

**Governor Rose Mofford**
**Taking the Oath of Office**
**Credit: The Phoenix Newspapers, Inc.**

**Governor Mofford**
**Working in her Office**
**Credit: The Phoenix Newspapers, Inc.**

state, Governor Bolin was originally reluctant to appoint Mrs. Mofford, but the backing of her friends from her 35 years in state government brought about her appointment as secretary of state.

Upon her ascension into the secretary of state's position, the character of the office changed dramatically as kachinas, various types of hats, and an array of plaques took over to fill the office. There was much more than just these physical signs of a change. Rose Mofford brought a personal style, work ethic and level of conscientiousness to the office that included her now famous returns of telephone calls, responses to the mail, and her penchant for keeping and being on time for appointments. Mrs. Mofford once said, "I try never to be late. I make it a point to leave in plenty of time. I don't want to get the reputation of being late. A woman has a harder row to hoe in some ways. You can't let people think you are all hot and bothered."

During her years as secretary of state, she was well known throughout the capital complex as a tall friendly woman with a "hive of spun white hair atop her head like a crown" and a sense of humor. She was known for her long days and receptiveness to the public whether in the form of office tours or in addressing concerns about rising taxes. She described her work as the secretary of state as follows:

"I work every day like I was running for re-election and the race was tight. That's the only way I know how. That's what my mother taught me."

Re-election was not an issue in spite of Mrs. Mofford's perceptions. She was re-elected to the secretary of state position in 1978, 1982 and 1986, winning a majority in all of the state's fourteen counties in each election. In addition to running her office, which was uniformly referred to as a tight ship, Mrs. Mofford served as President of the National Association of Secretaries of State from 1982-1983 and was known among that group as a leader in the processes of running a secretary of state office.

At the time of her election to a third term as Secretary of State in 1986, Evan Mecham became the first Republican governor in twelve years but yet it was his election that would propel Mrs. Mofford into a new job and state and national prominence. Governor Mecham experienced tremendous turmoil during his short administration that resulted in several different actions that directly impacted Rose. First, a recall movement was begun against Evan Mecham and it was the responsibility of Mrs. Mofford's office to receive the recall signatures, verify the legitimacy of the signatures and schedule a recall election should the recall be successful.

The recall election was successful but Mrs. Mofford was to do more than simply process the signatures and schedule an election. At the same time the recall movement was gaining momentum, there were allegations about Evan Mecham's misuse of public funds, the failure to disclose a campaign loan and possible interference with a criminal investigation of a death threat. With these allegations being widely reported, the Arizona House hired a special counsel to investigate and determine whether there was a sufficient basis to go forward with impeachment proceedings against Governor Mecham. Additionally, Attorney General Bob Corbin secured a criminal indictment against Governor Mecham.

The house special counsel did recommend impeachment proceedings and after a hearing the house voted (46-14) to impeach Governor Mecham. It was at that point that Rose Mofford was surprisingly changed from the routine life of secretary of state to the state's hectic life of the chief executive officer. The impeachment vote came after 5:00 p.m. on Friday afternoon, February 5, 1988 and confusion existed over the long holiday weekend as Arizona wrestled with the first-time question of who was governor between the time of impeachment and the time of the Senate trial for impeachment. Mrs. Mofford returned to her home on that Friday evening still unclear as to whether she would continue as the secretary of state or become the acting governor.

Within two days, it was clear that Rose Mofford was Governor Mofford at least until the pending impeachment trial in the Senate was held. When asked about her role as acting governor during Mecham's impeachment trial, her response was that her job was to keep the ship of state stable during her stewardship. She also expressed concern for the Mechams and the state during what was a confusing and dark period for the state.

Evan Mecham was impeached by the

**Governor Rose Mofford**
**Credit: The Phoenix Newspapers, Inc.**

181

Arizona Senate in April, 1988. After a few weeks as acting governor, Rose Mofford was the governor. Upon the vote, Rose Mofford issued a simple statement:

"Members of the press and my fellow Arizonans. This is a difficult hour in our state's history. My heart goes out to the entire Mecham family. Today, we have reached the end of some difficult times in Arizona. I know the decision made by the Senate today was not reached lightly. It is time to put all that behind us and move forward. Today our constitution has worked. Our elected representatives have spoken. As we work together to bind the wounds of the last few months, let us purge our hearts of suspicion and hate. Today, none of us are Republicans, none of us are Democrats. We are all Arizonans. Let us go forward together as Arizonans. I ask all of you for your prayers and your support, both for me and the Mecham family. I did not ask for this burden. But I do not shrink from the job before me. With God's help, I will not let you down."

Mrs. Mofford's goal was stability and few dispute that she brought a level of calmness and professionalism as she assumed the office. Her greatest challenge was putting together a staff and filling vacant government positions because she had such a short time to make the transition between offices. She was able to put together a staff of volunteers almost immediately. That temporary and volunteer staff, consisting of the best and brightest of Arizona, worked diligently with her to put together a permanent staff and their efforts were offered because of their respect for Rose Mofford. As Governor Mofford worked, some confusion still prevailed as the state tried to sort out the relationship between the recall election which had already been scheduled and the impeachment which had removed Governor Mecham from office. The questions that arose were whether the recall election must still be held and if so, whether Rose Mofford could run in the election. The Arizona Supreme Court eventually issued a decision that held the recall was called off since the purpose of removal had been accomplished by other means. The effect of the decision was to leave Rose Mofford in office until 1990.

Governor Mofford's administration has been almost universally described as one with a tremendous calming influence. The turbulence and emotional upheaval of the impeachment and recall were eliminated as Governor Mofford quietly took the reins and removed controversial appointments and restored order to the operation of state government. It was a quick career change which required the quick action so natural to Rose Mofford.

Once the honeymoon was over, Governor Mofford was beset with the usual, and sometimes unusual, trials of political office. For one, she fell backward off a platform at a speech in Yuma and because of a concussion was forced to spend a significant amount of time recovering. She was thrust into the lobbying efforts for obtaining a super collider project for Arizona and was criticized when Arizona's efforts were labeled as "amateurish."

The suddenness of her new job and the required time for development of a new staff left little time for long range planning and resulted in some criticism from those who demanded an agenda from Governor Mofford. Her administration continued in "limbo" until her first state-of-the-state address in January, 1989, in which she came out with a proposed budget, a statement of issues and a new forcefulness that left no doubt as to who was in charge of the state. Her address and attitude reinstated the faith of her party and others in her ability to govern the state.

During her administration, her primary emphasis has been on the importance of education and the need for adequate funding for schools and universities. Her philosophy has been that a proper educational system will bring Arizona to national prominence and allow its economy to grow and attract further investment.

Her work days have continued at the pace of the past as she labors to compromise with a legislature struggling with the severe budget deficits caused by a lagging economy. In the midst of all the ongoing work came the usual questions of seeking re-election which were answered by Rose with a firm "Yes" but which also brought former Governor Mecham back into the picture as an announced candidate.

As of this writing, Governor Mofford is one year away from a re-election campaign that promises to be challenging and colorful as she pursues public office and for the fourth time faces the state-wide electorate. When

183

asked how she would like to be remembered, she expressed her love for her work and state by saying "she was the governor who loved her state and would die for it."

## SOURCES

*Arizona Republic*—February 6, 1988, A6,
  March 4, 1988, A10,
  April 6, 1988, A1,
  April 8, 1988, A1,
  May 15, 1988, B1,
  June 12, 1988, B1,
  July 29, 1988, C5,
  August 5, 1988, B1,
  August 18, 1988, A1,
  October 2, 1988, B2,
  November 10, 1988, A3,
  December 7, 1988, B1,
  December 11, 1988, A1,
  December 16, 1988, B1,
  December 21, 1988, C1,
  January 1, 1989, C4,
  January 3, 1989, B1,
  January 9, 1989, A1,
  February 1, 1989, B8
Governor Rose Mofford, Personal Interview
*Mesa Tribune*—October 12, 1987, B1,
  January 9, 1988, A13,
  February 15, 1988, B1,
  February 21, 1988, B1,
  February 25, 1988, B1,
  March 7, 1988, A1,
  July 13, 1988, B1,
  August 12, 1988, A8,
  January 15, 1989, D3
*Phoenix Gazette,* November 22, 1977, C1
*Arizona Silver Belt*, People

# PATRONS

# CHANEN CONSTRUCTION COMPANY, INC.

**Herman Chanen**
**Founder of Chanen Construction Company**

Chanen Construction Company, Inc. (**CHANEN**) was formed in 1955 as a general building contractor and currently serves as Construction Manager (CM) and/or General Contractor (GC) on the many projects in which the company is involved. Our objective has always been to provide a full range of professional construction-related services. The intimate knowledge of construction methods and their relationship to costs, and the willingness to investigate and research innovations and ideas for the benefit of the building team, have provided savings of millions of dollars for hundreds of satisfied clients.

With corporate headquarters in Phoenix, **CHANEN**-built multi-million dollar industrial, commercial and institutional projects are in evidence from the east coast to the west coast. In the United States, our company ranks 108th in the "Top 400 Contractors," as reported in the May 1989 issue of *Engineering News Record*.

More than eighty-five percent of the company's annual volume is performed under the negotiated, construction management concept wherein CHANEN personnel provide extensive design and construction phase services structured to minimize the total required cost and completion time of each project and to ensure that quality levels are attained. The balance of our contract volume is performed under lump sum contracts secured through competitive bidding. Whether we are competitively bidding work as a GC or taking competitive bids from trade contractors on construction management projects, this activity in the bid market permits us to continually maintain an outstanding relationship with numerous trade contractors and suppliers. These bidding procedures enable our company to receive continuous input on the current cost and availability of the various existing and new systems and components that go into a project.

We believe that the key to the success of construction management is in the ability of the CM to recognize and perform certain design and construction phase services. These services include quality control, as well as cost and schedule control. Our Project Control System encompasses every facet of project management utilizing an experience team capable of performing all services required.

While all of the principals of our organization lend their respective expertise to **CHANEN**-built projects, they also function as a team to manage the growth and development of the entire company.

In addition to the key principals, an administrative staff of more than 60 specialists is involved in directing or performing the following functions: project management, estimating, value engineering, scheduling, cost control, quality assurance, field supervision, planning and design review, administration, data processing, corporate financial management and accounting.

Our employees continually demonstrate their ability: to manage the total process of project delivery, to communicate effectively, to complete projects on time, to complete projects on or under budget , and to be innovative.

**Performance is the major objective of our company.**

# TOM CHAUNCEY

**Tom Chauncey**
**Credit: Scott Trees Photography**

In 1926, a 13-year-old lad decided to leave Dallas, Texas, for new challenges and opportunities in the infant state of Arizona. Lacking funds to travel west in the conventional manner, he hopped a freight train and arrived in Phoenix with six pennies in his pocket.

After surviving the action and adventure in the town, Tom Chauncey stepped inside the Adams Hotel. He secured a job as a pageboy. This job kept him fed and gave him a place to sleep. A year later, at 14, with advice from then Senator Carl Hayden, Tom left the Adams to apprentice as a jeweler for Nathan Friedman, one of the leading jewelers in Phoenix. In the late 1930's, a young Chauncey opened a small jewelry store, Tom Chauncey Jewelers, later recognized as one of the finest jewelry stores in the Southwest.

This was followed by the success of six radio and two television stations in Arizona. With Chauncey as chairman of the Board, president and chief executive officer, KOOL-TV was to become the most successful television station in the state and a bellwether station of the CBS Network. Tom was elected chairman of the CBS television affiliates association and was a member and/or officer of 11 broadcasting industry organizations, always seeking to further his community and state's best interests.

He also found time to turn his attention to purebred Hereford cattle and to Arabian horses. He established the Clear Creek Cattle Company, which now controls nearly 300,000 acres of ranch land in Arizona. At about the same time, Tom founded Tom Chauncey Arabians, the famous Arabian ranch in Scottsdale, Arizona. Generally recognized as the father of the Arabian horse industry as we know it today, Tom still lives on his horse ranch on Scottsdale Road.

It is said by those who know him best that Tom Chauncey is a truly selfless man, a self-educated, self-made, superb businessman who became a successful community leader by serving others. He is a warm, friendly human being with depth, understanding and compassion.

Tom is less well known for his political activity. A long-time friend of President and Nancy Reagan, Tom had close ties with most of the political leaders of our state. He has known every governor in the state's history, all of our senators and congressmen. He was campaign manager for Ernest McFarland's successful run for the governorship. Named Ambassador to Nigeria, he was President Eisenhower's personal representative, along with Nelson Rockefeller, to the ceremonies marking Nigeria's independence from Great Britain.

In 1983, Arizona State University conferred an Honorary Doctorate of Humane Letters for the many contributions to the community and the state he served for all of his adult life.

Tom is a man who has accepted his responsibilities in community life. He has worn the mantle of leadership easily, gracefully, and humbly. Tom Chauncey: jeweler, broadcaster, rancher, public servant and humanitarian.

Tom Chauncey will say he is just a man. Others say he is a just man.

## INTERGROUP OF ARIZONA—
## AN HMO SUCCESS STORY

**Rick Barrett, President and CEO of
Intergroup of Arizona**

Intergroup of Arizona—ranked among the fastest growing companies nationwide and serving 160,000 members—is a far cry from the fledgling firm that organized in 1979.

Back then, two of Tucson's oldest and largest group practices—the Thomas-Davis Medical Center and Tucson Medical Associates—agreed to proved a new kind of medical delivery system. The idea was to provide quality medical care while controlling rising health-care costs.

That idea has blossomed into the Intergroup of today—a company thriving in the extremely competitive health care field.

Intergroup is one of a handful of physician-owned HMOs in the country. This arrangement has allowed physicians to maintain independent practices, which ensures our ability to deliver high quality medical care.

Intergroup has a commitment not only to treat members when they're ill, but to help them stay healthy. It offers members free health education classes, discounts at health clubs throughout the state, healthful information in quarterly newsletters and access to a new program called Health Risk Appraisal.

The Company also has a deep commitment to Arizona and its people. The company is a longtime supporter of community organizations such as the March of Dimes, Arizona Lung Association, the Arizona Theater Company and American Cancer Society.

Intergroup is headed by Rick Barrett, President and Chief Executive Officer. Mr. Barrett is a native Tucsonan who has lived in Arizona most of his life.

His charge is to manage the delivery of top-notch health care while containing costs—and ensure that Intergroup's success and tradition go hand in hand.

## KPNX—TV

**The Office of KPNX—Channel 12**

Phoenix had its first look at Channel 12 in 1953. Thirty-six years, and many "firsts" later, KPNX -TV continues to be a broadcasting pioneer in the Valley of the Sun.

KPNX (formerly KTAR-TV) was the first station in the Valley to broadcast in color in 1955. Television had already become regular family entertainment. As time passed, television's popularity continued to increase. As people began to watch daily, they also began to expect more from this new media.

Phoenix continued to grow and thrive and KPNX continued to grow with it. Changes and improvements were important to meet the increased expectations of viewers. One of those changes was the appearance of Sky 12. A news helicopter gave Channel 12 news an immediacy that made an impression. The unique microwave system used in Sky 12 gave Arizonans an opportunity to see, live, many of the events and places in the news.

In 1987, KPNX began a technical conversion to the MII videotape format. MII provides a sharper picture for viewers than other broadcast video, as well as being smaller and more portable (an advantage for news

coverage). KPNX was the first station in the country to adopt this new format, following the lead of its network partner, NBC.

Channel 12 News at 10 PM was the first daily newscast in Arizona to be closed captioned for the hearing impaired. By early 1989, the station had expanded its service to the hearing impaired community when real-time closed captioning was introduced. This captioning method uses trained court reporters and computer aided transcription equipment. The captioners listen to each newscast, adding the captions as the newscast airs, with only a 3-5 second delay. KPNX also expanded the number of newscasts captioned. Today every 5,6, and 10 pm newscast on KPNX is accessible to the hearing impaired—a total of 18 newscasts each week.

Phoenix and the Valley of the Sun have grown tremendously in the last three decades. KPNX is keeping pace with that growth, adapting to the ever-changing market through state-of-the-art technology and dedication. It's a commitment to Valley viewers that will continue well into the future.

# KARSTEN MANUFACTURING CORPORATION

**Karsten and Louise Solheim**

Karsten Solheim didn't know he would revolutionize the golf industry in 1958 when he examined the mechanics of putter construction and came up with a design for a superior putting instrument. Employing a heel and toe weighting design, which was the beginning of what is now know as "perimeter weighting," Solheim took an idea of "building a better putter" and transformed his dream into one of the leading golf manufacturing companies in the world. And it all began in a garage in Redwood City, California.

Today his company Karsten Manufacturing Corporation (KMC), and its subsidiaries employ more than 1,700. The executive offices and assembly plant, along with subsidiary Karsten Engineering, occupy 15 acres in North Phoenix. Other subsidiaries located in Phoenix include Moon Valley Country Club, a foundry (Dolphin), and two heat treating facilities (Sonee, Maximet). Suquamish Inc. is located in Suquamish, Washington, near Seattle.

This is truly a family-run company. Karsten's wife, Louise, acts as executive vice president while sons John, Allan and Louis serve as vice-presidents. Daughter Sandra is also involved in the operation of the company.

Solheim and his family were transferred to Arizona in 1961, while working for General Electric Computer Division as an mechanical engineer. He first started golfing at age 43, and his enthusiasm lead him to craft his own putter as he strove to improve his handicap.

The PING putter was named after the sound made by the original model 1A when it struck the ball. New models were added and became successful when leading golf touring pros won tournaments with the distinctive looking putters. As sales of the custom-made clubs increased, he resigned from his job at General Electric in 1967. His facility was moved into a small building on 21st Avenue and Desert Cove in North Phoenix. On June 30 of that year, the company incorporated and was named Karsten Manufacturing Corporation.

Karsten's reputation of producing superior golf equipment, such as putters, irons, woods, bags, balls, apparel and accessories has made it a leader in the golf industry. PING golf products are used by golf professionals and amateurs worldwide, and are exported annually to 70 countries including Japan, Europe, New Zealand, and South Africa.

Solheim's dedication to the art and science of golf has made significant contributions to our nation's economy as well as to the State of Arizona. In May, 1988, the corporation was honored by President Ronald Reagan and received the President's "E" Award in recognition of the outstanding export growth produced throughout a four-year period. In December, 1988, KMC received the Arizona Association of Industries Award for its efforts within the state.

What started out as an innovative way to make his golf game more successful in the garage of his home now spans the globe. With foresight, determination and devotion to his dream, Solheim gave his personal touch to the sport of golf. The PING ring became the sound of success.

# MOTOROLA'S PRESENCE IN ARIZONA

**The First Motorola Facility
in Arizona on North Central Avenue**

On February 4, 1949, a small article in a Phoenix newspaper announced that "The Motorola Radio Co., Chicago, has leased quarters and begun assembling a staff for a research laboratory in Phoenix." Few, if any, of the newspaper's readers that day had any idea of the ultimate impact of that event on the Valley's future economic and industrial development.

Dr. Daniel E. Noble, who died in 1980, was the person responsible for bringing Motorola to the Valley. He was impressed with Phoenix because it was a "clean city, with good schools, and an intellectual aura of growth and progress." He also felt "the Arizona climate was a great drawing card in the recruitment of the best qualified engineers and scientists." Noble came to be known as the "Father of Arizona Industry" and the Science Library at Arizona State University was named in his honor.

Two major divisions of Motorola grew out of the small Arizona group led by Noble.

The Government Electronics Group (GEG) is a premier producer of complex communications, radar and tactical electronic equipment for defense and space applications. GEG equipment has been employed on virtually every U.S. manned and unmanned space flight.

The Semiconductor Products Sector (SPS) produces more than 50,000 different kinds of semiconductor components—ranging from simple transistors to mind-boggling "computers-on-a-chip."

From its beginnings as a team of five engineers and technicians in a small 6,000 square foot laboratory, Motorola Inc. has grown to become Arizona's largest private employer with 21,000 employees working in thirty-eight facilities (nearly five million square feet) throughout the Valley.

# PHELPS DODGE CORPORATION

**Phelps Dodge General Office
Circa 1905**

**Phelps Dodge
Corporate Offices
1989**

Phelps Dodge Corporation with its corporate headquarters in Phoenix, Arizona, operates in 23 countries worldwide. Founded in New York in 1834 as an import/export firm, Phelps Dodge is one of the oldest corporations in America and this year it will observe its 155th birthday.

Operations began in Arizona in 1881, a full 31 years before Arizona became a state. This relationship, now more than 100 years old, began when Phelps Dodge and Company, the New York import/export firm that was the predecessor of Phelps Dodge Corporation, decided to consider copper mining in the West. Dr. James Douglas was commissioned to evaluate mining properties at Morenci and Bisbee, thereby laying the groundwork for what was to become the leading copper mining company in the State. Today, Phelps Dodge is North America's largest copper producer.

In 1988, Phelps Dodge produced about one-third of the copper mined in the United States. Using that copper, and copper purchased from others, the Company is the world's leading producer of continuous cast copper rod, the basic feed for the electrical wire and cable industry. Silver, gold and molybdenum are produced as by-products of the copper operations and fluorspar and small quantities of gold, silver and copper from mines abroad.

Phelps Dodge investments include a 44.6 percent interest in Black Mountain Mineral Development Company (Pty.) Limited, which operates a lead-silver-zinc-copper mine in South Africa. Exploration for metals and minerals is conducted in this country and abroad.

Phelps Dodge is still primarily a copper company, however, recognizing the importance of diversification, the Corporation acquired Accuride, the major North American producer of steel wheels and rims for heavy trucks and Columbian Chemicals Company, the world's second largest producer of carbon black—an essential ingredient in tires and other products such as printing ink and copying machine toner. Phelps Dodge is also one of the world's largest producers of magnet wire and has investments in companies that produce wire and cable products in 14 foreign countries.

# THE PHOENIX NEWSPAPERS

**Business Office Arizona Republican
Circa 1914
Credit: Oliver King**

With the help of Arizona Governor Lewis Wolfey and his supporters, *The Arizona Republican* made its debut May 18, 1890.

Heralding the agricultural development of the Valley of the Sun, *The Republican* enjoyed continual growth over the years.

In fact, less than a decade after its first issue, the straightforward and vigorous *Republican* purchased its competition. On June 1, 1899, it absorbed the *Salt River Herald*, the territory's first newspaper.

Not surprisingly, by 1920, *The Republican* had become Arizona's largest circulation newspaper—a position it holds proudly to this day.

On November 11, 1930, *The Republican* changed its name to *The Arizona Republic*. A mere seven days later, it combined publications with its biggest rival—*The Phoenix Gazette*.

*The Phoenix Gazette* was first published October 28, 1880, under the banner of *The Arizona Gazette*.

It was founded by Charles H. McNeil and W. D. Frazee—two energetic businessmen who did everything from gathering the news and setting the type to selling advertising space and distributing the newspaper.

*The Gazette* teeter-tottered between morning and afternoon publication, but by the 1900's, *The Gazette* established itself as an afternoon newspaper and boldly crusaded for progress—including a vocal campaign for a mainline railroad.

*The Gazette* combined operations with *The Republic* in 1930. Although published jointly, the two newspapers continue to maintain separate—and highly competitive—editorial operations.

Interestingly, the founders of the daily *Arizona Business Gazette* also established the *Arizona Weekly Gazette* in 1880.

A century later, Arizona's oldest weekly newspaper changed its name to the *Arizona Business Gazette*.

Published Fridays, the *Arizona Business Gazette* today is the state's largest circulation business and legal newspaper.

*The Arizona Republic*, *The Phoenix Gazette* and the *Arizona Business Gazette* were purchased on October 18, 1946, by the late Eugene C. Pulliam, founder of The Society of Professional Journalists, Sigma Delta Chi.

Characterized by a history of growth and prosperity, the newspapers broke ground in 1947 for a new building at 120 East Van Buren Street.

From this site, *The Republic, The Gazette* and *The Business Gazette* have grown steadily.

In fact today, the business of publishing these newspapers involves more than 2,300 full-time and 500 part-time employees, as well as a satellite printing plant, three branch offices and a newsprint warehouse.

*The Arizona Republic, The Phoenix Gazette* and *The Arizona Business Gazette*—a dynamic story of growth from territorial newspaper to major metropolitan newspaper.

# JUNE SCHMIDT

**June and Jacob Schmidt**
**Credit: Gittings Photography**

June Schmidt is the wife of Jacob Schmidt, a native Kansan, born and reared in the heart of America. Through hard work and perseverance, he started his own meat packing plant in the depths of the great depression. For thirty years the Kansas City Dressed Beef Company, of which Jacob was president and owner, did business all over the world.

His company survived the 1951 flood when three rivers converging in Kansas City over-flowed their banks and twenty-five feet of water engulfed the plant. Cattle went floating downstream with some even landing on roof tops. Carloads of beef ready for market were washed off railroad tracks. Despite this adversity, his company never experienced a month in the red.

Jacob spent a lifetime in community affairs having served for many years as a director at Security National Bank and as a member of the board of directors at Trinity Lutheran Hospital in Kansas City. He was president of the Greater Kansas City Industrial District, served on the Board of Governors for the American Royal, was president of Indian Hills Country Club, and president and elder of Immanuel Lutheran Church.

June Schmidt, nee Rice, was born in Salem, Massachusetts, but spent her formative years in Cambridge where she used to walk home from high school via the yard (Harvard). Eventually she lived in California, Oregon, Washington, Missouri and Kansas. She married, raised a family and taught psychology and family relations in the public schools where she also served as a counselor. An elected committeewoman for eight years she enjoyed politics and serving in related community affairs.

In 1978, the Schmidts were lured to the Valley of the Sun—Arizona, and this has been their home ever since.

## SOUTHWEST AIRLINES

**Southwest Airlines
Boeing 737—300 Jet Aircraft**

Southwest Airlines, the airline that almost two decades ago proved that low fares, high scheduled frequency and excellent attention to the customer's needs was a guarantee for success, brought its brand of service to Phoenix in 1982.

In the years since Southwest started service to the Valley of the Sun, the airline has grown to become the nation's ninth largest carrier and more than 1,400 employees call the Phoenix area home. The airline has an annual payroll of more than $56 million and, in addition, spends more that $101 million locally on the purchase of goods and services.

Starting with a fleet of three planes and 150 employees, Southwest Airlines has grown to more that 7,000 employees and will have 100 Boeing 737 aircraft with annual sales approaching $1,000,000,000 by 1990. At 5.3 years, the Southwest Airlines fleet is the youngest of all the regional, national and major carriers in the United States.

Phoenix is home for Southwest Airlines' state-of-the-art reservations center, which each day handles 30,000 incoming reservations calls.

In addition to being an active business force within the community, Southwest has also been active in community affairs promoting such activities as Scrooge Busters, which was recently instrumental in providing Christmas tree lights for downtown Phoenix.

# VALLEY NATIONAL BANK OF ARIZONA

**Valley National Bank's First Office**

**Valley National Bank Center Phoenix, Arizona Credit: Markow Photography**

I. E. Solomon knew the time-honored formula for business success: Find a need and fill it.

As a small-town storekeeper in remote southeastern Arizona during the late 1880s, he saw a definite need for a bank to serve a scattered but growing population. With support from 14 investors, he gathered $25,000 in capital to launch the Gila Valley Bank. Opening in January, 1900, it attracted copper miners, cattlemen, and farmers who handed hard-earned dollars to a clerk behind a desk set up at the rear of Solomon's store. Thus was born the financial institution that became Arizona's largest —Valley National Bank of Arizona.

From this promising beginning the new institution grew quickly, expanding to nearby towns and establishing the first trust department in the state. By 1914 it was profitable enough to rescue the ailing Valley Bank in Phoenix, although eight years would pass before the two were combined as Valley Bank and Trust, with $10 million in deposits.

Like other financial institutions in the United States, Valley Bank prospered during the 1920s. But from 1929 to 1933 deposit balances dwindled from $17.7 million to $6.7 million. The bank president, under the strain of those early Depression years, resigned. The directors asked Walter Reed Bimson of Chicago's Harris Trust to assume the helm.

On January 1, 1933, Bimson met with Valley Bank employees and made a historic declaration: "Make loans! Plain people need to borrow small sums for all kinds of purposes. Those people will pour into our bank if we convince them we're here to help them."

"Make loans" and "help plain people" were to be Bimson's guidelines for nearly 40 years. The bank recovered and began to grow again. In 1935 it acquired Consolidated National Bank of Tucson, the first financial institution in the nation to sign up with the Federal Deposit Insurance Corporation.

At the same time, Bimson enlisted the bank in the FHA home loan program, boosting Valley Bank to fifth in FHA loans in the nation—a major reason for Arizona economic recovery. His staff designed several other unprecedented programs: installment loans, car loans, education loans, loans for medical bills, and others. By the late 1940s this innovative bank had become the 75th largest in America, with deposits of more than $200 million.

During the following decades the institution took an active role in building Arizona by providing funds for agribusiness, manufacturing, construction, and tourism. Before Bimson retired in 1970, Valley Bank introduced direct deposit of Social Security checks and the first plastic charge cards.

A holding company, Valley National Corporation, was formed in 1981, with Valley National Bank as principal subsidiary. Under current leadership, the corporation has grown to more than $11 billion in assets, with over 200 offices state-wide.

# WESTERN SAVINGS

**When Western Outgrew its First Office
They Moved to 51 North 1st Avenue.
The Building Remained Standing Until
1988**

It was May 21, 1929 when Don C. Driggs and his sons joined B. C. Straughan to charter Western Building and Loan Association. Five days later, they officially opened their doors on the eighth floor of the Security Building in downtown Phoenix.

Determined to overcome an evolving Depression, the Driggs began to canvass Arizona, selling savings certificates in rural mining communities, reservations and railroad towns. A year later, the Driggs were able to purchase Straughan's stock to become full owners of the fledgling association.

Throughout the 1930s, Western employees worked hard to help the company prosper. During the first half of the 1940s, the company became Western Savings and Loan Association and moved to ground floor offices at 51 North 1st Avenue.

The association launched its branch in 1954 when it opened a "satellite" office in Mesa. The branch network grew at a steady pace, adding sites throughout the Valley including Scottsdale, Chandler, Tempe and Maryvale. By 1963, Western had fourteen (14) offices and by 1980, featured fifty five (55) locations.

Western was among the first financial institutions in the country to introduce "supermarket banking" by offering full-service branches inside Smitty's stores. The concept, begun in 1973, proved to be a major success for the company.

Western has also been one of the leaders in single family residential lending in Arizona, making its first mortgage loan in 1930. The company estimates it has made tens of thousands of home loans through the years, with plans to help even more families fulfill the dream of home ownership in the years to come.

# HERITAGE PUBLISHERS

**Dr. John L. Myers and Karen K. Kroman
Heritage Publishers, Inc.**

Dr. John L. Myers realized that for each person their life is most important. From that understanding and belief, Myers founded Heritage Publishers and Historical Publishers, a non-profit 501(c)(3). He believed there would be a significant market for publishing books that have historical value for individuals, organizations, corporations, communities, sports organizations, and books which preserve history for people with different ethnic origins.

*Personal—family history books* are written for the purpose of preserving family legacy and genealogical history. The story is researched through interviews with the individual, family, relatives, and friends—documenting the individual's activities, experiences, and purpose of life. It is written in a format that directly reflects the individual as they wish to be remembered—their legacy. Upon approval by the client, the book is printed and bound professionally with copies produced for distribution to family and friends.

*The organizational or historical books* are contracted for the client who wishes to publish a non-fiction or fiction book. Heritage Publishers has produced publications for Indian Tribes, universities, businesses, sports

organizations, city and state governments. Clients may choose either black and white or full color, 8 1/2 by 11 or 6 by 9 inch formats, softback or hardback with custom designed jackets. These books are published for clients throughout the United States and in foreign countries. Books require 9 months to 2 years for completion depending upon the specific project. When completed, the books are often given as presentation pieces to valued clients, visiting dignitaries, or as special awards and sold retail. In addition to writing history-documenting books, Heritage prepares annual reports, marketing brochures, and other business documents.

In 1989, a new publication will be released by Heritage Publishers entitled, *Your Life Story, A Step-by Step Workbook* An easy to use, step-by-step workbook with easy to answer questions, the book assits the individual to document his or her own life for family enjoyment for generations to come. Inclusive in this manual are questions that generate the responses that make it easy to write their own story and to select their favorite photographs that would enhance their book. A 60 minute audio tape is included in the manual that gives first-hand experience as relayed by clients who have also completed their life history. This workbook will be appropriate for individuals of all ages and backgrounds. It will be a great gift for special occasions or any time one wishes to acknowledge a family member or a friend.

The professional staff of Heritage Publishers has background in writing and publishing all types of publications. All publications are produced with "state of the art" computer equipment. Professional and personal service, attention to detail, and pride in the finished product are the primary reasons that the future looks bright for Heritage Publishers. Although Heritage Publishers has grown to include accounts for large corporations and national organizations, we believe we have not forgotten that it is the value of each individual life that makes our business successful.

# INDEX